COMPLETE BOOK
OF
MULTIPLE DEFENSES
IN
FOOTBALL

COMPLETE BOOK

OF

MULTIPLE DEFENSES

IN

FOOTBALL

S.E. SULLINS

Parker Publishing Company, Inc.
West Nyack, New York

© 1978, by

PARKER PUBLISHING COMPANY, INC.

WEST NYACK, N.Y.

Library of Congress Cataloging in Publication Data
Sullins, S   E
  Complete book of multiple defenses in football.

  Includes index.
  1. Football--Defense. 2. Football coaching.
I. Title.
GV951.18.S9   796.33'22   77-20076
ISBN 0-13-158196-1

DEDICATION

To my wife and partner, Diane, our children, Darrell, Lynne, and Johnathan, my mother, Della, and my father, the late R.C. Sullins. Thanks for a debt I will never be able to repay. Your encouragement and support have been priceless.

ACKNOWLEDGMENTS

This book was developed for coaches and students of the game of football. A number of ideas presented within the text have been gathered from different people with whom I have been associated in high school and college football.

I would like to take this opportunity to thank the coaches for whom and with whom I have worked during my career. A special thanks to all the football players with whom I have had the pleasure of coaching. You taught me a great deal more than I taught you.

WHAT THIS BOOK WILL DO FOR YOU

This book takes into consideration the limitations placed on coaches, particularly at the high school level, in regard to size of staff, teaching load, time, and the number of participants. It is with this thought that I have tried to carry you from the basic defensive plan up and into the multiple defense package.

The objective of this book is to show how multiple defenses can be used to stop modern offensive systems. A team that uses only one defense is at a disadvantage against modern offensive formations. The defense should keep the offense off balance by utilizing a multiple scheme. If the defense can make the offense unsure of whom to block, it has a definite advantage.

This book shows how to perfect a multiple defense that forces offensive mistakes to happen . . . how to place personnel where their talents can best be utilized . . . how the multiple scheme can be a time-saving device each week as you prepare for opponents that utilize varying offenses . . . how to be a step ahead of your opponents' offenses by forcing them to work on all defensive sets while you specialize in a few . . . how to conceal your defense so the quarterback cannot effectively use audibles.

It also shows how the total defensive package stems from one basic defense . . . how to show different alignments but still retain simplicity . . . how to control the Veer series from both the Wishbone and Pro formations . . . stunts that render the triple option useless . . . how to defend against the Winged T series with the multiple scheme . . . how to defeat the power plays from the 1 formations . . . how to control the passing game of an opponent that utilizes the pro passing attack . . . how to develop hard-nosed defensive players through the use of multiple drills . . . how to use multiple incentives to develop an enthusiastic, helmet-busting defensive unit.

In addition, there are detailed diagrams of each defensive set, stunt, or drill used to teach the multiple defensive scheme. I have tried to explain each maneuver so that portions can be incorporated into any system with a minimum of confusion.

The multiple defensive package has been tried and proven effective in major colleges and small high schools with limited staffs and a small number of participants. Millport High School of western Alabama, which has 2 coaches and 25 participants and utilizes multiple defenses, won back-to-back championships in the West Central Alabama Conference with records of 8-1-1 and 8-2. During this period, Millport High School was ranked 5th and 8th in the state in Class A.

Mississippi State University, using a basic 4-3 Defense, finished last in the Southeastern Conference in total defense and compiled a record of 4-5-1. In the next season, we utilized the multiple defensive scheme as described in this book, with excellent results: an 8-3 season record, a Sun Bowl Victory, and a ranking of 17th in the nation by the A.P. and U.P.I. polls. In the following year, Mississippi State finished the season as the number two team in total defense in the strong S.E.C. and as one of the top twenty defensive teams in the nation. The record for the next season was 9-2, with a ranking of 18th in some polls. During these three seasons, the State defense has produced four All-Americans and one athlete who was named the Most Valuable Defensive Player in the Southeastern Conference. The multiple defensive scheme has provided our ballclub with the edge needed to compile winning seasons back to back.

All coaches agree that sound fundamentals, good defense, and the ability to avoid mistakes are the ingredients that produce a winning season year after year. If two teams are comparable in ability, sooner or later the defense and/or the kicking game will decide the contest. A multiple defensive team has an edge over a team that uses only one basic defense, because the former can place strength against strength and the best personnel at the point of attack.

S. E. Sullins

Table of Contents

CHAPTER 1

BUILDING MULTIPLE DEFENSES
FROM THE 50 DEFENSE

There will always be controversy over the two predominant theories in defensive football. One approach is to major in one defense and perfect it to the utmost, using a number of stunts that are well concealed. The other approach is to limit the number of stunts used, but present several different alignments.

There are advantages and disadvantages in each. An advantage of the first is that a team can work on the minute details of each position. A disadvantage is that the offense will be able to pick apart the same defense play after play. An advantage of the second is that the offense will have to do some thinking on the line of scrimmage and possibly make a mistake; e.g., a missed assignment or a poor play selection. A disadvantage is that if a number of defenses are used, the different techniques will be poorly learned because of the limited amount of practice time.

I believe that a middle-of-the-road philosophy should be utilized. One major defense should be perfected, and a limited number of other defenses should spring from the techniques learned in the basic defense.

It has always been my contention that the defense is not the absorbing unit; rather, it should be the unit that forces mistakes. The defense should at times surprise the offense and attack the offensive system. The defense should never sit in one alignment and let the offense probe until the weak spots are located. If the defensive players are sold on the multiple package, they will always feel that they are a step ahead of the offense. By my standards, a good defensive team is one that plays technique well, utilizes the big play people, and keeps the offense off balance.

THE 50 DEFENSE

There are several reasons why the 50 Defense was chosen as the starting point upon which to build the multiple defensive package. The 50 Defense has five anchor points, points where a defensive lineman can make immediate contact with and neutralize an offensive lineman. The 50 Defense has four defenders in the secondary, whereas some other defensive schemes utilize three. The secondary coverage can be well concealed prior to the snap of the ball. I also feel the 50 Defense has two other very good advantages: It is a good stunting defense, and it is flexible enough to cover any offensive set.

SELECTION OF PERSONNEL

In the multiple defense, the selection of personnel is more important than in any other scheme because of the different techniques employed at certain positions. There should be consideration given to the placement of the "Big Play" people and where they can best be utilized. The majority of offensive teams are predominantly right handed, and this should be given top priority when you are placing your better defensive personnel.

Nose Guard—One of your three best players; quickness and toughness should be prevalent. This player should have the athletic ability to play in an up or down position. Size is not of great importance, but the player should have average or above average strength. Many high schools effectively employ a 170-175 pound nose guard. This position is the key to the multiple defense.

Left Tackle—The left tackle should be one of the better players on the squad; he is a cornerstone of the defense. He should be right handed because the greatest percentage of the blows he will deliver will be with the right shoulder and flipper. This position should be filled by a player who stands 6′1″ or better and weighs 190 pounds or more.

Right Tackle—The right tackle can be slightly smaller than the left tackle. The majority of high schools have only one really good defensive lineman. This player should be on the left side. The right tackle can be an average player with good technique. The right tackle should be a good athlete because the right side is harder to play than the left side if a player is right handed. If a team has a defensive lineman who is left handed, he should be played in this position because of the contact with the left shoulder and flipper.

Anchor End—This spot should be filled with a tough, hard-nosed youngster because this position will get a lot of action. He must have enough strength to close the off-tackle hole and the agility to take on a blocker and still contain the quarterback. At times, he will be asked to play pass defense, but this should be secondary to his play against the run. His size can range anywhere from 5'10", 170 pounds, to 6'3", 210 pounds. A defensive tackle with agility can sometimes play this position.

Rover End—The rover should have average speed, be able to read formations, and have the ability to play man to man coverage against a back. Strength is desirable, but not as important as quickness and the ability to get to the ball. The rover end must also be able to contain the quarterback on run-pass options. The rover end is very similar to a linebacker. His size in high school can range from 5'10", 165 pounds, to 6'1", 195 pounds.

Sam Linebacker—The strong linebacker, or Sam, should be placed in the same category as the nose guard. He should be an excellent football player with intelligence. He should have above average size, good speed, and the ability to deliver a blow and shed blockers who are larger than himself. He should be able to read offensive formations and check defenses on the line of scrimmage since he will be the defensive signal caller. Sam linebackers in high school can range in size from 6'0", 185 pounds, to 6'2", 210 pounds.

Willie Linebacker—The weak side linebacker, or Willie, should have above average speed and quickness. He must be able to run with a back on man to man coverage and have the quickness to execute stunts effectively. Willie should also have a knowledge of formations and complement Sam in the ability to read offensive tendencies. He should be able to shed blockers and be an excellent hitter. This is a spot where you can play a youngster who goes to the ball well but lacks technique. His size can range from 5'9", 165 pounds, to 6'1", 205 pounds.

Strong Safety—The strong safety should have very good speed, excellent feet, the ability to play pass coverage, and the strength to take on the run. He will be called upon to play up front in certain alignments, and he needs the emotional make-up of a linebacker. In high school, the strong safety can range in size from 5'9", 160 pounds, to 6'1", 195 pounds.

Free Safety—The free safety should be the center fielder in the secondary. He must be able to prevent a score if a back pops free and no one else has a chance to tackle him. He must be one of, if not the, fastest men on the team. The free safety must have a knowledge of formations and know the pass responsibility for each secondary position. The free safety should fall into the category of the Sam linebacker and nose guard. He must be one of the best athletes on the squad.

Right Corner—The weak side corner should be the best 1 on 1 pass defender in the secondary since he will be called upon to defend against a split end quite a lot. He should have the ability to recognize bootlegs, counter passes, and reverses. He must be able to give support quickly from wide alignment. The right corner's size can range from 5'9", 160 pounds, to 6'2", 190 pounds.

Left Corner—This position is similar to the anchor end. The left corner will probably get more run action than the right corner. He needs fair size, the ability to get a jump on the ball, and the ability to read the routes of the receivers. He needs as much speed as possible, and he must be a sure open-field tackler. He must be able to support the run from a wide alignment and a tight alignment. Your best overall cornerback should be on the left side.

DEFENSIVE HUDDLE

The huddle is the beginning of each play in football. The offense is trying to guess what defense will be used according to past tendencies and the immediate situation. The defense is also anticipating the offensive play based on down, distance, and where the ball is located on the field.

The defensive huddle should be set up so that the entire defense, except for the signal caller, is facing the offensive personnel. The Sam linebacker should have an unobstructed view of his bench and of the coach calling the defensive signals.

At the conclusion of each play, the nose guard is responsible for locating the ball and setting the huddle three yards in front of it. The two cornerbacks should remain at their positions and check all substitutions coming on and off the field. Several times in the past seasons, we have seen a trick play designed to draw everyone into the huddle, at which time the offense would throw a long pass. In a game with Ole Miss this happened, and now we caution cornerbacks to double check all substitutions and be alert for this type of a play. (See Figure 1-1.)

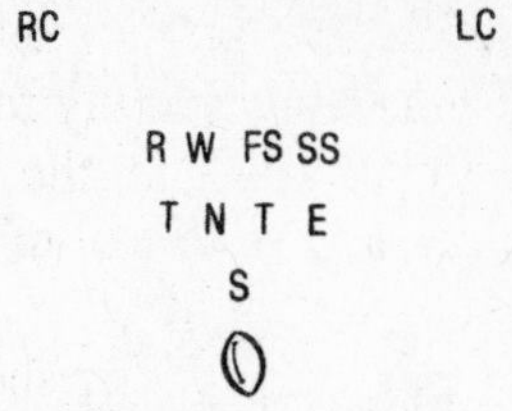

```
      RC                      LC


         R W  FS SS
          T N T E
             S
             ()
```

Figure 1-1

The Sam linebacker must receive the defensive call from the sideline, step into the huddle, and remind the unit of the down and distance situation. After this reminder, he can make the call for the front seven people. The free safety must call the secondary coverage to complement the forcing unit. After the calls are made by the Sam linebacker and the free safety, the command of "Ready" is given and the huddle is broken by everyone clapping his hands on "Break." An example of a huddle call would be: "50 Strong Dart, 50 Strong Dart, Cover 1, Ready, Break." The free safety should relay the call and the coverage to the cornerbacks since they didn't enter the huddle. This is done verbally or through hand signals.

After the huddle is broken, the players move to their respective positions. The nose guard and tackles should be on one knee in order to enable the linebackers and secondary to observe the offense as they break the huddle. Nothing can conceal offensive formations from the Sam linebacker better than a big, broad-shouldered tackle standing up just as the offensive players take their positions.

Sam must call the formation and strength as he moves to his alignment. If there is a question about the vulnerability of the defense against a certain formation, Sam may check to another call.

TECHNIQUES OF THE DEFENSIVE FRONT

The techniques that are employed in the multiple scheme are based on the numbering system made popular by Bear Bryant of

Alabama. A designated area on each offensive lineman is numbered and carries with it a certain stance, read, and technique. (See Figure 1-2.)

Figure 1-2

ANCHOR END

The anchor end is taught a 9 and standup 5 technique that will be utilized throughout the multiple scheme. He will flip-flop to the tight end side on the 50 and 70 Defenses. The anchor end always lines up to the left side if the 40, 80, or 53 Stack Defenses are called. If there are two tight ends, he plays on the strong side. If there is a slot and a split end, the anchor will move to the one receiver side. The anchor should line up with his outside foot back and his inside ear on the outside ear of the tight end, eighteen inches off the ball. His keys are the tight end and the near back. The release of the tight end should give him his first key. If the tight end blocks down, the anchor must take a short jab step with the inside foot and use either a shiver or a flipper to force the offensive end off his blocking path. (See Figure 1-3.) After he steps and hits, the anchor must take a short step with the outside foot and another short step with the inside foot in order to assume the original stance. If the tight end blocks down and the near back goes away, the anchor should close to the inside and look for a guard pulling to trap him. If the offensive end blocks down and the near back is coming toward him at an inside-out angle, the anchor must close using the inside pad. If the back's angle is to the outside leg of the end, the anchor must shuffle to the outside, keeping his shoulders square, and contain the quarterback. (See Figure 1-4.) If the tight end releases to the outside on a pass route, the anchor should get his hands on him to alter his release and locate the ball. On a drop back pass, the anchor should contain the rush. On a flow away, the anchor trails the play as deep as the ball. If the tight end releases to the outside and the quarterback comes down the line on the option, the anchor "feathers" the quarterback. The anchor should begin to chop his feet, always keeping the outside leg back. He will move down the line in this manner, staying slightly to the outside and approximately two yards from the quarterback. If the quarterback turns up inside, the anchor must push off the outside leg and tackle the quarterback with his head across the chest. If the quarterback pitches to the trailing back, the anchor should push off the inside foot and sprint to close down the seam between himself and the cornerback who has turned the pitch man to the inside. (See Figure 1-5.) The anchor end will on occasion be called to move down and play a standup 5 technique. The anchor has to play this technique in much the same way as the 9 technique. The only time anchor should be in this position is in a "revert" call. When he receives this call, he must take the dive man if the tackle blocks down. The anchor must align himself on the outside shoulder of the tackle and key him as he did the tight end when he was in a 9 technique. (See Figure 1-6.)

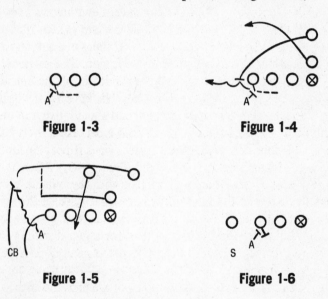

Figure 1-3

Figure 1-4

Figure 1-5

Figure 1-6

ROVER END

The rover end flip-flops to the open side of the formation. If there is a slot and a split end, he goes to the two receiver side. Against two tight ends, he should go away from the strong side of the formation. The rover end will be taught a 9 technique exactly like the anchor, a drop technique, and a standup 5 technique. The drop and the 5 technique will be the only two techniques covered, since the 9 has been discussed. The term drop tells the rover end to drop off the line of scrimmage in a two-point stance. This helps the end get a quicker read on the play and helps him get to the curl area if a drop back pass occurs.

Drop—The drop is played in conjunction with the 50 Defense against a split end. The rover end assumes a stance, with his feet parallel, approximately two yards outside of his tackle and two yards off the ball. His keys are the near back and the flow. If the near back and the flow are away from him, the rover must shuffle to the inside on cutbacks. (See Figure 1-7.) If the near back dives, the rover must be ready to take the quarterback on the option. If the near back is coming at an angle to block him on the sprint pass, the rover must shuffle to the outside, shuck the blocker, and contain the quarterback. (See Figure 1-8.) The rover must never commit to the cutback lane unless he is sure the counter option will not be run to his side. On a drop back pass, the rover and Willie should key the near back as they drop to their zone. If the near back blocks, the rover will remain in the curl zone and Willie will stay in the hook zone. (See Figure 1-9.) If the near back releases in a flare of flat route, the rover will begin to come off the curl zone and break to the back as the ball is thrown, and Willie will move to the curl area.

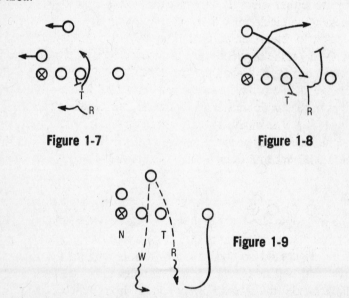

Figure 1-7   Figure 1-8

Figure 1-9

Standup 5 Technique—The standup 5 technique is played in conjunction with the 70 Defense. The rover end aligns himself eighteen inches off the ball and a yard from the weak side offensive tackle. His keys remain the same. He now becomes the trail man on a flow away, and he has no pass coverage. The responsibilities remain basically the same: on an option he has the quarterback; on a sprint out he must contain. If a "revert" call has been made by his linebacker, the rover must be tighter on the offensive tackle, and his responsibility will change to the dive if the tackle blocks down and the veer option shows.

TACKLES

Defensive tackles in the multiple scheme are taught four techniques. These are the 5, 4, 3, and 2 techniques. This may seem like a lot to learn, but there are really only two different techniques to learn. The 5 and 3 techniques are basically the same, and the 4 and 2 techniques are related.

5 Technique—The tackle should align himself eighteen to twenty-four inches off the ball, with his inside ear on the outside ear of the offensive tackle. The stance can be either a three or four point, with the inside foot staggered. The key is the offensive tackle and the blocker to either side. If the offensive man blocks down on the linebacker, the tackle must deliver a blow with the shoulder and force the blocker to release on an angle that will keep the backer free. (See Figure 1-10.) If the blocker uses a reach block, the defensive man must use either hands or a shoulder to flatten the blocker to the line of scrimmage. If the offensive tackle pulls to the outside and the ball is inside him, the tackle must squat and work back to the inside for a trap or a dive. If the defensive tackle receives a fold block, he must work across the face of the guard in order to squeeze the running lane. (See Figure 1-11.) When a double team occurs from the tight end and the

| Figure 1-10 | Figure 1-11 |

offensive tackle, the 5 technique must take a short lateral outside step and deliver a blow with the outside pad to the tight end. After contact, the inside foot must come up as the driving force in an attempt to split the double team. A defensive lineman should never be driven back into the pursuit lanes of the linebackers. The defender should drop to the ground if he can't split the double team. (See Figure 1-12.) When the offensive blocker drives for a turn-out block, the defensive tackle will bring up the inside foot and deliver a blow with the inside shoulder and forearm. The defensive tackle must stop the offensive blocker's charge and bounce across the face. The coordinated movement of the flipper and feet must be perfected. If the blocker is coming out high, the shoulder will be used; if the blocker is coming low, the hands will be used. (See Figure 1-13.)

   3 Technique—This technique will be discussed next because of the close relationship between a 3 and a 5 technique. The stance and alignment off the ball are the same in both techniques except that the tackle aligns himself over the shoulder of the offensive guard in the 3 technique. (In the 5 technique, the tackle was on the outside eye of the offensive tackle.) The key will be the offensive guard and the blockers to either side. The reaction to blocking patterns will be the same in the 3 and 5 techniques except for a reverse fold block. The tackle must read this, step to the outside, deliver a blow to the offensive tackle, and work across his face. (See Figure 1-14.)

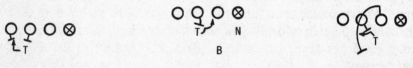

Figure 1-12   **Figure 1-13**   **Figure 1-14**

   4 Technique—The defensive tackle should align himself eighteen to thirty-six inches off the ball, with his outside eye on the inside eye of the offensive tackle. A three- or four-point stance can be used; the feet should be parallel and the weight balanced. The reactions to the blocking patterns will be almost identical to a 5 technique. The keys for the 4 technique are the same as for a 5. The tackle must realize that by aligning himself to the inside, the offensive tackle has a better blocking angle than on the 5 technique. On the snap of the ball in the 4 technique, the defensive tackle should take a short jab step with the outside foot and anticipate the down block. If the down block does not occur, he must read the blocking pattern and react.

   2 Technique—The tackle aligns himself on the inside eye of the offensive guard twenty-four inches off the ball. His keys are the guard and the adjacent blockers. The reactions to blocking patterns are basically the same as in the other techniques that have been discussed. The tackle should be aware that he is more apt to be trapped in this alignment than in any other. One block the 2 technique will see a great deal of, is the cutoff block by the center with a guard pulling. This block is the same as the fold block when the tackle was in a 5 technique. The tackle must react to the center and work across his face, locating the ball as he moves.

NOSE GUARD

The nose guard is taught to play four techniques. The 0 technique is used on the 50 and 53 stack; the standup 0 is used on the 40; the standup 1 technique is used in the 80 defense; and the 2 technique is used in the 70 defense.

0 Technique—The nose guard aligns himself head up on the center, taking all the ball he can get. He should key through the center's head to the quarterback. If the center's head leads to one side or the other, he should drive through the center's block, trying to flatten his body to the line of scrimmage and never allowing the center to get his shoulders past the nose guard. (See Figure 1-15.) If the nose guard reads a double team from one of the guards, he should drop the shoulder to the side of the double team and try to split the block. The nose guard can never be driven back into the pursuit lanes of the linebackers.

Figure 1-15

Standup 0 Technique—The noseguard is aligned head up on the center, two yards off the ball, in an upright position. The stance should be relaxed, with the knees flexed and the feet parallel. Key the center, the quarterback, and the fullback tandem. If the flow is to either side, fill outside your tackle. (See Figure 1-16.) If a pass shows, work the middle and the backside curl. If the center uses a cutoff block on one of the tackles and the quarterback is spinning, the nose guard should step up to avoid a blocker and close the gap. (See Figure 1-17.)

Figure 1-16   Figure 1-17

Standup 1 Technique—The nose guard should be aligned on the inside eye of the offensive guard to the tight end side, three yards deep, in an upright position. He should key through the guard to the near back. On a flow to his side, the nose guard must be able to fill outside the tackle and also step up to the inside if the back starts wide and breaks back. (See Figure 1-18.) On a flow away, he must check over the center for any cutback. On a drop back pass, the nose guard must take the strong curl or middle, depending on the formation.

2 Technique—The nose guard will be aligned on the offensive guard to the tight end side in the same manner as the defensive tackle. The reactions to blocking patterns will be the same for the nose guard as it is for the tackles.

SAM LINEBACKER

The Sam backer will be taught four basic techniques in the multiple scheme. The 7 technique will be used in the 80 and the 54 Defenses, the 5 technique for the 40 Defense, the 3 technique for the 50 Defense, and the 1 technique for the 70 Defense. Sam will also be taught a "revert" for the 40 and 80 Defenses. This is more of a coaching point than a technique.

7 Technique—Sam will align himself one yard off the ball and inside eye of the tight end. Sam will key the tight end and near back. If the tight end blocks down, Sam will jam the tight end and locate the ball. If the tight end releases and the flow is to Sam, he will scrape to the outside. (See Figure 1-19.) If the flow is away, Sam will work down the line of scrimmage for a cutback. In a drop back pass, Sam will work the onside curl or flat, depending on the formation and coverage.

5 Technique—Sam will align over the outside eye of the tackle to the tight end side, or strong side if the formation has two tight ends, and approximately three yards deep. Sam's keys will be the blocker in front of him and the near back. If the tackle blocks down and the near back dives, Sam will step up and fill. (See Figure 1-20.) If the tackle drives straight out, Sam will step up and use the inside shoulder to close the seam. On a drop back pass, Sam has the onside curl or flat, depending on the coverage called in the huddle.

3 Technique—Sam will play the 3 and 5 techniques almost the same. However, he will receive two different blocking looks when aligned over the guard: the fold block and the guard pulling. If the guard blocks out on the tackle, step up and be ready for the tackle folding inside. (See Figure 1-21.) If the guard pulls, take a step in that direction and locate the ball. If a drop back pass occurs, work the onside curl.

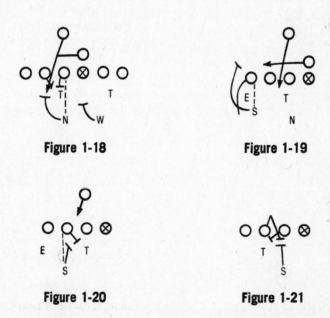

Figure 1-18   **Figure 1-19**

Figure 1-20   **Figure 1-21**

1 Technique—Sam will align to the tight end side, three to four yards deep, on the inside eye of the offensive guard. He will key through the guard to the near back. On a flow away, he will check the cutback over the center. (See Figure 1-22.) On a flow to his side, he will skate down the line of scrimmage behind his linemen, keeping leverage on the ball. On a drop back pass, he will cover the onside curl.

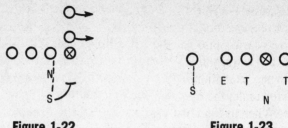

Figure 1-22   Figure 1-23

Revert Technique—This technique is used in the 40 and 80 Defenses when the linebacker gets a "flex" or an abnormal split by the tight end. We feel we must call a "revert" when the end gets a three-yard split. The defensive end will move down into a standup 5 technique, and the linebacker will move head up the tight end, two yards off the ball. We will play an inside eye position up to five yards, but if the offensive man goes wider we will stay at this point. The linebacker must feel the block of the end and key the ball. (See Figure 1-23.)

WILLIE LINEBACKER

The Willie will be taught four techniques in the multiple package. He will use a stack 0 in the 53 Stack, a 3 technique in the 50 Defense, a 5 technique in the 40 Defense, and a standup 1 technique in the 70 and 80 Defenses. The Willie linebacker will also be taught a "revert" technique that is identical to the play of the Sam linebacker.

Stack 0 Technique—Willie should line up one yard behind the nose guard in a good hitting position. He should key the back away from Sam and the flow of the ball. (See Figure 1-24.) Willie should anticipate the guard to the side of flow blocking down on him. On a drop back pass, he will cover the middle, looking for drag patterns.

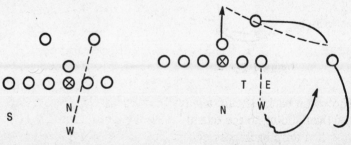

Figure 1-24   Figure 1-25

1 Technique—Willie will align himself to the split end side or to the two wide receiver side, three to four yards deep on the inside eye of the offensive guard. Willie's technique will be the same as Sam's.

3 and 5 Technique—The play is the same for both Sam and Willie, with the exception of the near back key on the pass that has been discussed under the rover end technique and the 5 technique in the 40 Defense. Whereas Sam had the curl in a 5 technique on a drop back pass, Willie must take the flat. (See Figure 1-25.)

SECONDARY PLAY

The secondary is the last line of defense between the offense and the goal line. These players must get a correct read on the ball and react as a unit. Our basic philosophy is a four-deep rotating secondary that features zone coverage. We do not feel that we can give up any passes, because a good quarterback will control the ball on the possession passes, such as the curl and flat routes. We want someone in all seven zones once pass action shows.

The four-spoke secondary can be compared to a wheel: as the ball moves to one side or the other, the spokes in the wheel will rotate in that direction. The spokes in the wheel must keep a relative distance away from each other as they rotate. (See Figure 1-26.)

When the ball stays inside the defensive ends, the spokes should collapse and squeeze down to the point of attack. (See Figure 1-27.)

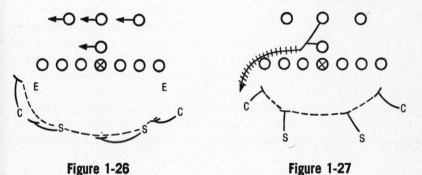

Figure 1-26   Figure 1-27

The cornerbacks should always be conscious of a back hitting inside and then sliding to the outside. (See Figure 1-27.)

If a drop back pass occurs, the wheel will expand as the spokes get depth. (See Figure 1-28.) Again, the relative distance between each position must be maintained. If one man in the secondary gets too much depth, there will be an area that is impossible to cover.

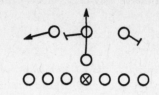

Figure 1-28

1 COVERAGE

Our basic coverage is what we refer to as 1 cover. We will flip-flop our strong and free safety because we want the strong safety to play run support more frequently than the free safety. The alignments and techniques for the 1 coverage are as follows:

STRONG SAFETY

The strong safety will play an invert position to the strong side, three yards outside of the tight end and seven yards deep against a pro formation. If there is a tight wing or a closed formation, the strong safety will align over the offensive tackle and ten yards deep. (See Figure 1-29.) The position of the strong safety is determined by the split of the flanker back to his side. If the flanker has more than a five-yard split, we would probably have the strong safety in a revert position. The keys for this position would be the tight end and the ball. If the tight end blocks down and the flow is to him, the strong safety comes to the line of scrimmage and turns everything to the inside. (See Figure 1-30.) If the ball goes away from him, the safety should rotate back through the deep third and be in position to cover the tight end. On a drop back pass, the safety works slowly back in the seam with his eyes to the inside, but if a receiver threatens the flat he jumps on him immediately. (See Figure 1-31.) The safety stays in the seam between himself and the cornerback if no receiver is in the flat.

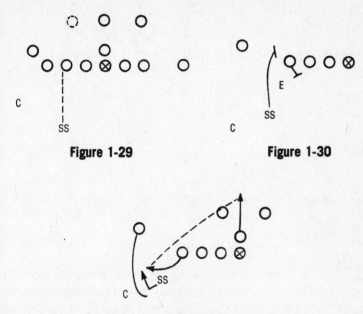

Figure 1-29   Figure 1-30

Figure 1-31

FREE SAFETY

The free safety is the quarterback in the secondary. He must be able to recognize formations and talk to the people around him. The alignment for this position in 1 coverage is over the weak side offensive guard-tackle gap, twelve to sixteen yards deep. The free safety will key the ball. If the ball goes to the weak side, he must be able to cover the split end on a take-off pattern. (See Figure 1-32.) If the wide receiver gets an abnormal split and the free safety doesn't think he can cover him deep, he should call or signal ''Invert'' to the cornerback on that side. This will put the free safety on run support to the weak side, with the corner covering the deep third.

On run action to the strong side, the free safety must work the middle third before he attempts to help on the tackle. As the safety works in the direction of the play, he must be alert for the post pattern by the wide receiver. (See Figure 1-33.)

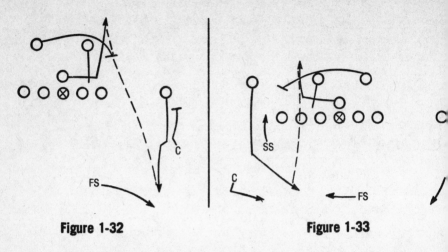

Figure 1-32   **Figure 1-33**

When the quarterback drops straight back to throw, the free safety should get depth and read the quarterback. The safety should remember where he is in relation to the sidelines and the favorite routes of the opponents.

CORNERBACKS

In 1 coverage, the cornerbacks will align over the wide receiver's outside eye eight to eleven yards deep. The cornerback to the strong side of the formation will play the deep third on a flow to him and help on the run when he is sure there is no threat of a pass. On a flow away from him, the strong corner will work his third before rotating across to support. (See Figure 1-34.) On a straight back pass, the strong corner takes the deep third to his side. If the offense has a closed formation, the cornerback to the strong side will be four yards deep and two yards outside of the flanker or end. (See Figure 1-35.) If run action shows his way, he must support, with the strong safety taking the deep third. If the flow is away from him, he must rotate back through the deep third. If a drop back action shows, the strong corner must take the flat to his side. (See Figure 1-36.) The weak corner, against most of the offenses we face today, gets to support on the run more often than the strong corner because not many offenses use a closed formation. In 1 coverage, the weak corner must be in a position to cover the deep third to his side and also support on the run his way. Against a closed or open formation, the weak corner must support on run to him unless an ''Invert'' call has been made. (See Figure 1-37.) If the flow is away,

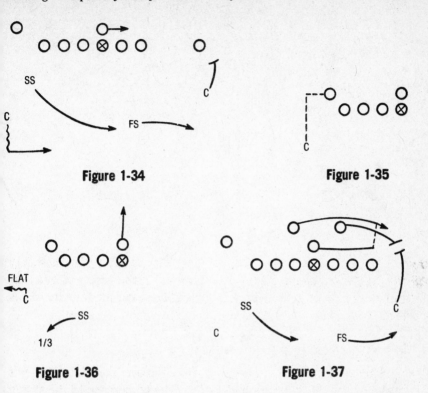

Figure 1-34

Figure 1-35

Figure 1-36

Figure 1-37

the weak corner must go to the deep third and cover any receivers. If a drop back pass shows, the weak corner will again go to the deep third because our rover end will take the curl and flat to his side. If the defense is facing a pro formation, the weak corner rules are basically the same as those used against a tight formation. The weak corner should be able to support the running game to the split end side. As the corner comes up, he should force the wide receiver inside to help the free safety. (See Figure 1-38.) If the flow is away from him, the corner will work the deep third as he rotates across. If a drop back pass shows, he must hang tough, with the receiver to his side. The weak corner should be alert for an over split by the end. Once he feels that he cannot close the seam between himself and the defensive end as he comes up to support on the run, he should give an "Invert" call to the free safety. This changes the responsibility for run support to the safety if action shows weak side. The weak corner now stays in the deep third, with the receiver to his side, and he plays pass until the threat of a run is established. (See Figure 1-39.)

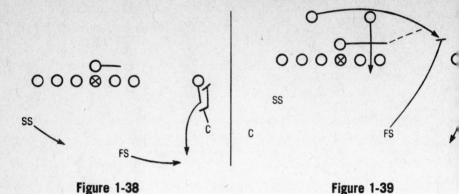

Figure 1-38   Figure 1-39

1 SWAP COVERAGE

When we call 1 Swap, it is usually in conjunction with the 80 Defense. 1 Swap coverage means that the secondary simply reverses the 1 coverage as far as alignment and run support to the split end side are concerned. Whereas the strong safety has run support to the strong side of the formation in 1 coverage and the weak corner had to come up on a run to the split end side, the positions are now reversed. The strong safety now has run support to the split end side. (See Figure 1-40.) With a flow to the strong side of formation, the corner has run support, with the free safety covering the deep third. (See Figure 1-41.) On a drop back pass, the cornerbacks will work the deep thirds to their sides and the free safety will work the middle third. (See Figure 1-42.)

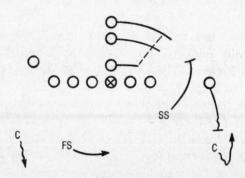

Figure 1-40

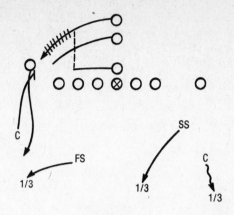

Figure 1-41

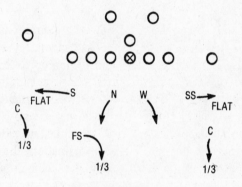

Figure 1-42

2 CALL

We utilize a zone call that helps our underneath coverage, and we get exceptionally quick run support from the cornerbacks. This coverage is called 2 cover. The secondary will align itself in the same manner as it did in the 1 coverage, but it will shift as the quarterback goes into his cadence. The corners will cheat up to a position on the outside shoulder of the wide receiver at a depth of four to six yards. The corners will bump the wide receivers and force them to release to the inside. As the corners force the wide outs to release inside, their eyes will focus on the next closest receiver. If no receiver is threatening the flat, the corner will slowly backpedal to close down the area between himself and the near safety. (See Figure 1-43.) If a receiver is releasing to the flat, the corner will start to work back and then come up to cover him. (See Figure 1-44.) If run action shows his way, the corner must operate on the outside shoulder of the blocker and squeeze the ball carrier down to the inside as much as possible. (See Figure 1-45.) On a run action away from him, a corner must force the receiver to release inside and check for any throwback patterns or reverses to his side.

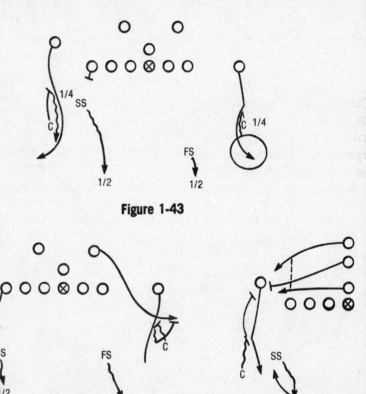

Figure 1-43

Figure 1-44   **Figure 1-45**

Both the strong and the free safety will drop to a depth of approximately eighteen yards and have the responsibility of covering half of the field to their side of the formation. (See Figure 1-46.) The safeties have no immediate run responsibility as such, but should go to the ball as quickly as possible once a running play is assured.

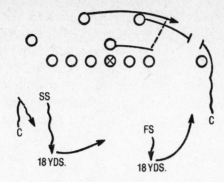

Figure 1-46

The underneath coverage will change somewhat from Cover 1 to Cover 2. Sam's responsibility will remain the same as in Cover 1, but the Willie backer now must hang in the middle for delays by the tight end or a back. The rover end will work to the curl and remain there regardless of what the near back does because the corner to his side has the flat. (See Figure 1-47.)

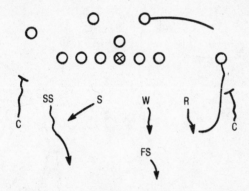

Figure 1-47

The hardest pass pattern to cover when a defense uses Cover 2 is when the wide receivers run a flag route to either side and the tight end runs a deep seam. When I was coaching high school football, one of the teams on the schedule was using a great deal of Cover 2. We decided to put in an audible system that would take advantage of this coverage. Each time our quarterback caught this team in 2 coverage, he would check off to the pattern shown in Figure 1-48. The success of this pattern against 2 coverage was evidenced by the fact that our quarterback threw three touchdown passes of over forty yards and we won by a score of 34-7.

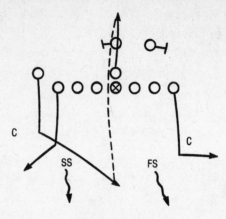

Figure 1-48

Some method of holding up the tight end and/or the wingback, or of having a linebacker in position to cover a receiver down the middle for a short period of time, should be devised. One way to help on this pattern to the tight end is shown in Figure 1-49.

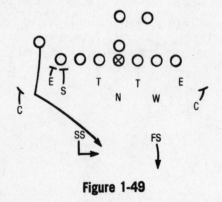

Figure 1-49

COVER 2 ROLL

In Cover 2, the cornerbacks will have the flat area to their respective sides regardless of the action of the ball. When Cover 2 is called, it tells the corners to stay in that area until all possible threats to their position are eliminated and then to go to the ball. When Cover 2 Roll is called, the cornerbacks will play the same on a drop back pass as they would on Cover 2, but if the ball moves to one side or the other the secondary will revolve as shown in Figures 1-50 and 1-51. The underneath coverage in Cover 2 Roll will be the same as in Cover 2.

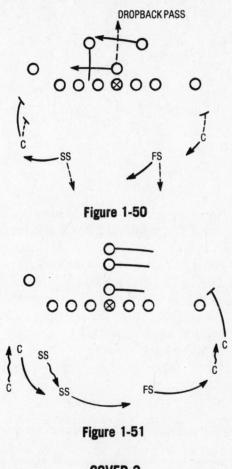

DROPBACK PASS

Figure 1-50

Figure 1-51

COVER 3

Cover 3 is used sparingly in our scheme, but it has its place in certain situations. If we want to play the 40 Defense with someone up tight on the wide receivers, we could use 3 Cover. (See Figure 1-52.) The corners have the deep thirds to their sides, and the free safety will work the middle third. The strong safety will take the flat as he did in 1 cover. Usually our alignment is deeper than when we are in 1 cover, but, again, we don't want to enlarge the seams between our underneath coverage and the secondary too much.

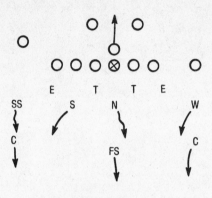

Figure 1-52

COVER 4 OR MAN COVERAGE

There are several ways we can play man to man coverage, but we will be concerned with two basic ways we utilize this coverage in our total package. One way to use man coverage is for the cornerbacks to take the widest receiver to their side, the strong safety to take the second receiver to the strong side of the formation, and the free safety to take the second eligible receiver to the weak side. (See Figure 1-53.) This scheme is used when we are in our 40 or 50 Defenses and we have a rush on the quarterback. If we feel the offense might try to slip the fifth eligible receiver out, we can pick him up with one of the ends or a linebacker. If an offense has a tendency to slip a back out of the backfield away from the side of the end that is covering him, we must put the Sam linebacker on the back and rush the end.

COVER 4-REVERSE

The Cover 4-Reverse is another scheme of man coverage used in conjunction with our 53 Stack or 80 Defense when the strong and free safeties swap sides. The free safety will now take the tight end man for man, and the strong safety will cover the tailback. (See Figure 1-54.) Again, we can pick up the fifth receiver with a linebacker or an end.

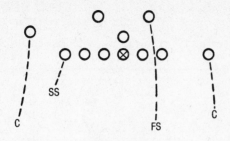

Figure 1-53

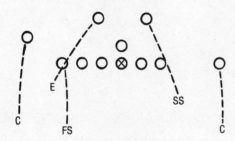

Figure 1-54

COMBO CALLS

Combo calls are utilized to give a quarterback trouble in reading the coverage and to help camouflage the 2 cover. The alignment for the corners in a combo call should be around eight yards deep on the outside shoulder of the receiver. The two safeties will line up over the offensive tackles' outside shoulders, twelve to fourteen yards deep. We will use two different combo calls: Combo Strong and Combo Weak. In Combo Strong, the coverage is almost the same as in 1 coverage for everyone but the strong safety and strong corner. The strong safety now has the deep third to his side if Combo Strong has been called, and the corner has the flat if run action or a drop back pass occurs. (See Figure 1-55.) If action shows to the weak side, the strong safety will work the deep middle and the strong corner has the deep third to his side. (See Figure 1-56.)

The linebackers in the combo calls will always work opposite of the strong or weak calls. If they hear a Combo Strong call, they know that if a drop back pass shows they must work to the weak side of the formation. Sam must work the curl to his side, the nose guard works the middle zone and weak curl, and the weak linebacker should take the assignment that the rover end has in Base 50. Willie keys the near back as he drops and breaks to the back as the ball is thrown.

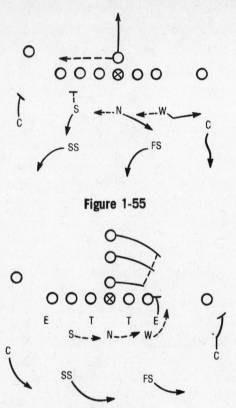

Figure 1-55

Figure 1-56

The Combo Weak call will be the opposite of the Combo Strong call. If run action shows either way, the secondary will revolve in the direction of the ball and the linebackers play their run keys. (See Figure 1-57.) If a drop back pass occurs, the Willie linebacker will work only the curl area and have no flat responsibility. The nose guard should work the strong curl, and Sam must take the strong flat. If a straight back pass develops, the weak side corner has the flat to his side and the free safety will work the deep third to that side. The strong safety will work the deep middle, and the strong corner will work the third of the field to his side. (See Figure 1-58.)

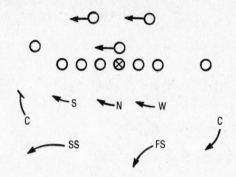

Figure 1-57

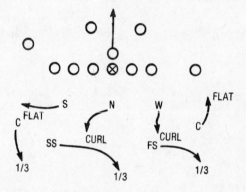

Figure 1-58

There are two points that should be stressed to the cornerbacks when you are using combo coverage. The first point is that the corner-back must force the wide receiver to release inside and/or alter his route in order to buy time for the safety to cover the deep third to his side when run action shows. The second point is that if the corner has the call to his side and a drop back pass shows, he should not go up to cover the flat if there is no threat. He should be in a position to take the receiver if he runs a quick out, but if the receiver pushes off the deep he should settle back to close down the seam between himself and the safety.

BASIC 50 STUNTS

The following stunts are taught to the defensive unit after the basic techniques have been learned. Stunts are not a cure-all for a defensive team, but they are good for breaking the rhythm of a drive and forcing the offense into a bad situation.

50 STRONG DART (See Figure 1-59)

Nose—50 alignment. Know where the strength of the formation is located. On the snap of the ball, take a short lateral step with the foot to the strong side and club the center with the onside hand. Be in a hitting position when you clear the line of scrimmage.

Sam—Know where the nose guard is darting. If he is darting to you, play deeper; if he is darting away, tighten up.

Will—Know where the nose guard is darting. If he is darting away, tighten up slightly.

S.T.—Play 50.

W.T.—Play 50.

Anchor—Play 50.

Rover—Play 50.

S.S.—Play coverage called.

F.S.—Play coverage called.

S.C.—Play coverage called.

W.C.—Play coverage called.

Note: Weak Dart is played the same way.

50 STRONG SLANT (See Figure 1-60)

Nose—Use the Dart technique to the side of the call.

Sam—Same as Dart. On a drop back pass, work the middle and weak side curl.

Will—Same as Dart. On a drop back pass, work the backside curl. As your go to the curl, key the near back. If he runs a flare or flat route, you must cover him. If the slant is away from you, take a lateral step to the inside and square up.

S.T.—If the slant is to you, take a lateral step to the outside, square up, and contain. If the slant is away from you, take a short jab step with the inside foot and drive through the guard-tackle gap.

W.T.—Same as strong tackle.

Anchor—If the slant is to you, drop to onside curl on snap of the ball. If the slant is away from you, trail.

Rover—Same as anchor.

S.S.—Play coverage called.

F.S.—Play coverage called.

S.C.—Play coverage called.

W.C.—Play coverage called.

Note: Weak Slant is played the same way with a change of assignments.

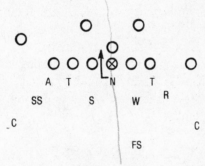

Figure 1-59

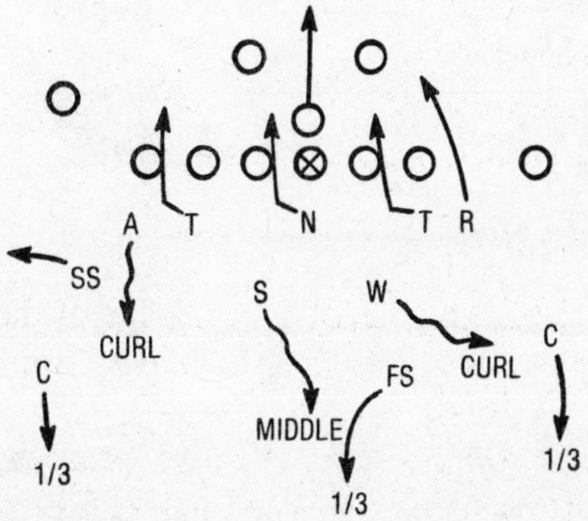

Figure 1-60

50 STRONG DART-CROSS (See Figure 1-61)

Nose—Execute a Strong Dart.

Sam—Key the near back. If the flow is to you, be able to scrape to the off tackle hole. If the flow is away, fill the weak side guard-center gap. On a drop back pass, you have the strong curl.

Will—Key the near back. If the flow is away from you, check for cutbacks. If the flow is to you, scrape outside your tackle. On a drop back pass, you have the weak curl.

S.T.—Execute a Slant technique to the inside.

W.T.—Execute a Slant technique to the inside.

Anchor—Play 50.

Rover—Play 50.

S.S.—Play coverage called.

F.S.—Play coverage called.

S.C.—Play coverage called.

W.C.—Play coverage called.

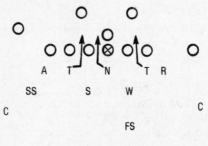

Figure 1-61

CHAPTER 2

COACHING MULTIPLE DEFENSIVE
RESPONSIBILITIES AND ALIGNMENTS

In any endeavor a group undertakes, the group must first decide on what is to be accomplished and the route to be taken. All good defensive teams have objectives that are stressed by the coaching staff and ingrained into each player's thinking. The objectives that are stressed by the defensive staff at Mississippi State are listed below.

DEFENSIVE OBJECTIVES

1. *Don't let our opponents score.* Each time we take the field, our defense is aiming for the ultimate: a shutout. If our oppositions don't score, we can't lose.
2. *Score on defenses.* We want to score while our offense is on the bench. Our defensive unit must be capable of switching from defense to offense instantly. We want interceptions, blocked punts, safeties, and punt returns to achieve this objective.
3. *Prevent the big play.* We must not let our opponents have a pass completion or a run of over twenty yards. We must not receive penalties. In the kicking game, we must be perfect.
4. *Limit the offense.* If a defense is playing well, they will limit the offense to three yards or less per carry. When this is achieved, you should win. We want to turn the ball over to our offense in a good field position. We don't want our offense to have to drive eighty yards to score.

5. *Force mistakes*. There are several ways in which a defense can force an offensive mistake. Pursuit and gang tackling are two of the better ways to demoralize a team and cause fumbles. Shifting defenses can cause poor play selection on the part of the signal caller and result in a costly mistake. The kicking game plays a very important part in our thinking when we attempt to force mistakes.

6. *Pride*. In order to have a good defense, the players must believe that through hard work they can be the best. Each person must take pride in developing the techniques needed to win. When you reach the point at which every man on defense believes in the rest of the unit, your defense will be hard to beat.

COMPILING A DEFENSIVE GAME PLAN

In any defensive game plan, several things should be considered. We must be sound against all formations and plays, and our Base 50 must be equipped with certain stunts that will break the rhythm of an offensive drive. We must also decide what other defenses in our package will place our personnel in positions that will better enable them to stop the offense of our opponents. We want to concentrate our defensive plans on stopping the following offensive features:

1. The formations and favorite plays from each. Some teams will use certain formations to pass from, and others will be utilized for the run game.

2. The five or six favorite run plays, regardless of formation and which back is the "money" player. Some teams will emphasize the tailback, and others the fullback or quarterback.

3. The five most often used pass plays. A team usually will go to certain players or pass patterns when faced with a critical situation. We want to be able to defend against these perfectly when the time comes.

4. Down and distance tendencies. We must anticipate plays in certain situations: first and 10, second and 6, third and 5, and so on.

5. The favorite short yardage formations and plays and which player has the highest percentage of carries in each situation.

6. Goal line offensive pattern. Most teams have two or three

plays that are used primarily inside the ten yard line. We must be prepared for these plays and also know whether the offense has a pattern of running outside or inside, throwing inside or outside, and, on a fourth down, kicking the field goal or going for the touchdown.

7. Hash mark tendencies. If an offensive team tends to go to the wide side of the field, we can utilize this information to our benefit.

We want to stop the best things an offensive team has done in the past, and we feel we need more than one defensive look in order to be successful. For example, if we are to face a team that features the 1 formation with the sprint pass or run, a trap, and the toss sweep as their best plays, we might emphasize the 50, the 40, and the 80 Defenses.

After we know the plays we must stop, we will organize practice to achieve the desired results. In the individual periods, we will work on the individual blocks and pass routes we anticipate facing in the upcoming game. In the group periods, we will work on reading the blocking patterns by the front and the combination routes by the linebackers and the secondary. We will have a stunt period at least twice a week, and a goal line defense will be featured three times a week, interspersed between the group and team periods. Our kicking game is last on the agenda, and the importance of it is stressed.

During our team periods, we want to check out all defenses, stunts, and coverages. If we find that we are unsound in some area, we must cancel that particular stunt or make an adjustment. In the team periods, we also stress field situations and opponent tendencies. In some instances, we may have to check out of one defense against certain formations. During the team periods, we want to make sure the players are exposed to the checks.

If we use the 50, the 40, and the 80 Defenses against the sprint pass or run, we could defend effectively with the defenses shown in Figures 2-1, 2-2, and 2-3.

In Figure 2-1, we show the 50 Defense used against the sprint.

In Figure 2-2, the sprint out is shown against the 40 Defense. When our Mike backer reads a definite sprint out, he will scrape off the tackle and close the seam between himself and the defensive end.

In keeping the responsibilities as closely tied together as possible in each defense, we also use the scrape method by the nose guard or Mike backer in the 80 Defense. Once he reads definite sprint out, or when the quarterback gets behind where the tight end originally lined up, Mike scrapes. (See Figure 2-3.)

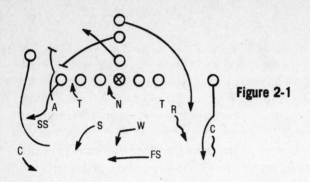

Figure 2-1

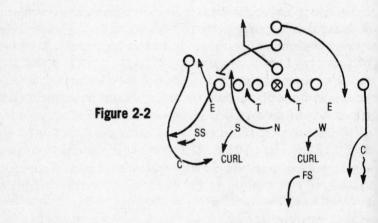

Figure 2-2

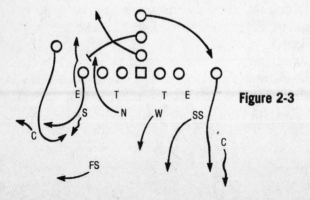

Figure 2-3

Figures 2-1, 2-2, and 2-3 are examples of a part of a game plan that we could use against a team that used the sprint out effectively. We would use this same train of thought in setting up other parts of the game plan.

SHIFTING DEFENSES

A defensive team has an advantage over an offensive team since they do not have to be set for one full second before the ball is snapped. This advantage can be exploited to the fullest if careful consideration is given to the placement of personnel. We do not want a player to move more than a step or two when we are changing our defensive looks.

Practice time must be allotted to the perfection and timing of the movement of defensive fronts. The timing of movement is very important because if you move too quickly a good quarterback will check off to a play that may hurt the defense you move into. If you move too late and the ball is snapped as you are moving, the defense will be exposed and seams will develop because your people are not ready to take on blockers and read their keys properly. The key to shifting defenses is the Sam backer knowing the quarterback's cadence, and once he passes the check off point the defense should be moved by a defensive signal. Often a defense such as the 80 Defense should be shown to the offense and then the players should move back to the Base 50. Consideration should also be given to the offense going on a quick count. A defense should be prepared to play the defense they are lined up in. For example, if "50 move 40" is called and the ball is snapped on the first sound, the defense should play 50. The game plan should not call for shifting defenses each play since movement on every snap can use up quite a lot of energy on a hot, humid day.

Each and every defense has its strengths and weaknesses, and we want to camouflage these until the very last moment. Whenever we can make the offense unsure of whom to block, we have a tremendous advantage. When an offensive lineman tries to read the defense and loses his aggressiveness coming off the ball, we feel that we have the upper hand on the line of scrimmage.

40 DEFENSE

The 40 Defense originated several years ago, and Greasy Neale, former head coach of the Philadelphia Eagles, was the person who popularized this scheme and called it the Eagle Defense.

The Eagle Defense, as known to most coaches, consists of four linemen, three linebackers, and a four-deep secondary. This defense was primarily a passing defense early in its existence, but, with a few adjustments in recent years, it is now very strong against the run. The adjustments that have been made to the Eagle are: the nose guard is farther off the line of scrimmage and can scrape to either side of his tackles, the tackles play a 2 technique rather than a 3, and the linebackers' positions are different.

The 40 Defense will be moved into from the 50 Defense when our Sam backer gives the word. The only players who move are the tackles, the nose guard, and both linebackers. (See Figure 2-4.)

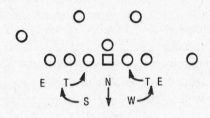

Figure 2-4

The secondary will play zone coverage as described in Chapter 1 and a combo coverage. The combo coverage will be used primarily with the 40 Defense and can be called to either the strong or weak side. If the call in the huddle is "40 Defense, Combo Strong," the secondary will be revolving to the strong side of the offensive formation on a drop back pass and the linebackers will work to the weak side of the formation. The cornerbacks will line up eight yards deep and over the wide receiver's outside shoulder. The inside safeties will line up ten to fourteen yards deep and over the offensive tackles. If run action shows, the secondary will rotate in the direction of the ball.

The responsibilities for the 40 Defense are as follows:

Anchor End—Will always line up to the left side regardless of formation and play a 9 technique. If the end splits three yards or more, listen for a "revert" call from your linebacker. If you get the call, move down and play on the tackle's outside shoulder as you would an end.

Rover End—The rover will always line up to the right side regardless of the formation. The rover end will have to play the "revert" call with the Willie linebacker in the same manner described for the anchor end. Rover has no pass coverage responsibility; he is committed to rushing the passer.

Left Tackle—The left tackle will move head up on the offensive right guard and play a 2 technique. Neither tackle should allow the offensive linemen to over-split them and create an area that is too large for the nose guard to cover. If an over-split occurs between the guard and center, the tackle should move back off the ball and read the guard and center.

Nose Guard—This player will drop back off the line of scrimmage and play a standup 0 technique. The nose guard will take either middle hook or weak curl, depending on coverage.

Right Tackle—The play of the right tackle will be identical to that of the left tackle.

Sam Linebacker—The strong linebacker will align over the strong side offensive tackle in a standup 5 technique. Sam must be alert for an abnormal split by the tight end and move to the "revert" position. Sam will work either strong side curl or flat on pass coverage. Sam will key the block of the offensive tackle and the release of the near back.

Willie Linebacker—This linebacker will align over the weak side offensive tackle in a standup 5 technique. Willie must be alert for a three to four yard split by the end to his side and play the revert call as described for the Sam linebacker. Willie will key the block of the tackle and the back nearest him.

Secondary—The defensive secondary can and will play any of the coverages that have been described. Coverages that will be utilized with the 40 Defense are 1, 2, man, and combo coverage.

THE 53 STACK DEFENSE

The 53 Stack, as we will refer to it, has been very effective for us against different offenses. This defense is the age-old 53 Defense that was used successfully against the single wing teams in another era. (See Figure 2-5.) We have changed some of the techniques employed by the front seven people, but the alignment remains basically the same as in a 53 Defense. The 53 Stack, has been used successfully by high schools, colleges, and pro teams. Colbert County High School in Leighton, Alabama won an Alabama 3A State Championship utilizing the defense shown in Figure 2-6.

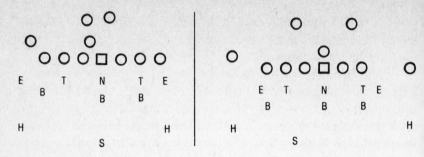

Figure 2-5   Figure 2-6

The Kansas City Chiefs in the 1960's, and more recently the Miami Dolphins, used a form of the the 53 Defense that is very similar to the 53 Stack that we employ. Most pro teams that employ the 53 Defense play zone coverage and rush only three players, as shown in Figure 2-7. The pro teams usually substitute a linebacker for a defensive lineman in passing situations.

Shifting from the 50 Defense into the 53 Stack is very simple. The only positions that require movement are the Sam and Willie linebackers and the defensive tackles. The strong and free safeties will exchange positions once the offense breaks the huddle. The Sam linebacker moves to a standup 7 technique, Willie must stack behind the nose guard, and the tackles move to a 4 technique. (See Figure 2-8.)

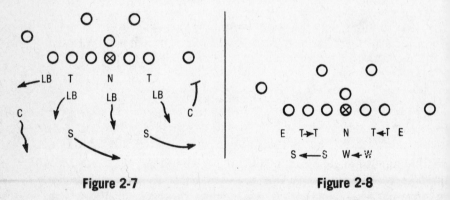

Figure 2-7   Figure 2-8

The responsibilities for each position in the 53 Stack are as follows:

Anchor End—This end will always line up on the left side regardless of formation. He will play a tough 9 technique on the outside eye of the offensive end.

Rover End—The rover end should assume a position on the right side of the defense regardless of the type of formation. He must play a 9 technique if he has a tight end to his side. If there is a split end to his side, he stays up on the line of scrimmage in a similar position. The rover end will play in a drop position on certain calls in the 53 Defense. When the rover is on the line of scrimmage, he has no pass responsibility except to rush. When the rover is in the drop position, he covers the flat or curl, depending on the coverage called in the huddle.

Left Tackle—Both tackles must move to a head up or to what we call 4 technique and read the offensive blocking pattern.

Nose Guard—Play a normal 0 technique.

Right Tackle—Play a 4 technique.

Sam Linebacker—Slide to a standup 7 technique on the tight end. In the event there are two tight ends, Sam plays to the end on the strong side of the formation. (See Figure 2-9.) If there is only one tight end and a slot formation, Sam plays to the weak side of the formation. (See Figure 2-10.) Sam will key the block of the tight end and the release of the near back. On a drop back pass, he will have the near back man for man or work the near curl, depending on the coverage called in the huddle.

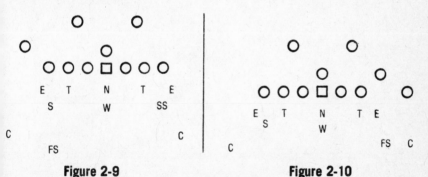

Figure 2-9   Figure 2-10

Willie Linebacker—This backer plays in a stack position behind the nose guard and keys the flow of the ball and/or the back away from Sam. If the offense is in the split back formation, Willie will key the tailback. If the offense is in the 1, Willie should key the fullback. On drop back passes, Willie should work the middle hook area or the weak side curl, depending on the coverage.

Strong Safety—The strong safety's alignment will depend upon the coverage called. If man coverage is indicated, the strong safety must always go the split end side and take the near back as shown in Figures 2-11 and 2-12. If there are two tight ends, the strong safety should go the the weak side of the formation and take the nearest back. (See Figure 2-13.)

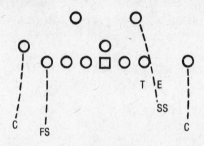

Figure 2-11

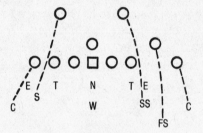

Figure 2-12

Figure 2-13

Free Safety—The free safety will play in his normal alignment unless 1 Swap is called, in which case he works to the tight end side. If man coverage is called, the free safety must go to the two receiver side of the formation and take the second eligible receiver. (See Figures 2-11 and 2-12.)

Cornerbacks—The corners on both sides have the first receiver to their side in man coverage. If a zone call is utilized, the cornerbacks will play the alignment as described earlier.

53 STACK SPECIAL

We will play the 53 Stack with zone coverage in order to keep the quarterback from throwing the post pattern and other routes that are good against man coverage. We attempt to give the quarterback the same look regardless of whether we are in 53 Stack, 53 Stack Special, or the 53 Prevent, which will be discussed in a later chapter. All players are in the same alignment as in the 53 Stack with man coverage, but the difference is that we are not rushing six players as we do in the 53 Stack. We will rush four people and drop seven to cover all zones. We must use the 1 Swap coverage when we run the 53 Stack Special. (See Figure 2-14.)

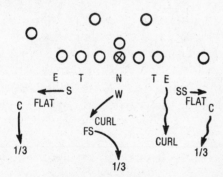

Figure 2-14

THE 70 DEFENSE

The 70 Defense is a defense that is ideally suited to what we refer to as a "situation defense." Once a breakdown on an offense is secured, there will be certain situations in which an offense will be likely to run only one or two formations. The 70 Defense can be called when the defensive team anticipates an open formation. An open formation is an offensive set in which there is a split end and the defense has got to cover only seven areas along the front, as shown in Figure 2-15.

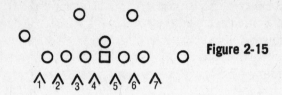

Figure 2-15

The 70 Defense is a combination of two very good defenses. The 70 Defense combines the best features of the 50 and 80 Defenses. Shifting from the 50 Defense into the 70 Defense is relatively easy because of the limited number of people who move to a new alignment. The nose guard, weak side tackle, and rover end are the only ones who will move as much as a yard. The two linebackers will adjust themselves only slightly since they are almost in position when they take their normal 50 alignment.

The responsibilities for each position in the defense are as follows:

Anchor End—This end must go to the tight end ride and play a normal 9 technique unless a special call puts him to the split end side, where he will play a standup 5 technique. On a straight back pass, he must contain the quarterback as he rushes.

Rover End—The rover must play to the split end side and has no pass responsibility except to contain a rush unless a special call puts him to the tight end side. If he gets the special call, he will work the curl.

Left Tackle—If the tight end is to your side, play a normal 5 technique. If the split end is to your side, move down to a 3 technique on the offensive guard.

Right Tackle—You have the same responsibility as the left tackle.

Nose Guard—Line up in a 0 technique and locate the tight end. When you get the command to move, slide to a 2 technique on the offensive guard to the tight end side.

Sam Linebacker—Check the offensive team as they leave the huddle, and if they do not have a split end check back to Base 50. If the offense has a split end, let the quarterback go into his cadence and move the defense once he gets past the check off point. Your alignment will be on the inside eye of the offensive guard, to the tight end side, three to four yards deep.

Willie Linebacker—Help the Sam linebacker check the formation when the offense breaks the huddle. Move to the split end side of the formation and align yourself in a standup 1 technique, on the inside eye of the offensive guard, at a depth of three to four yards.

Secondary—The secondary will not be affected by the movement of the front seven people. It always plays its normal alignment and coverage unless a special call has been built into the game plan. Coverages that can be used with the 70 Defense are 1, 2, 2 Roll, and man.

THE 80 DEFENSE

The 4-4 Defense, or 80 as we refer to this particular alignment, came into prominence several years ago. The 80 was a takeoff on the old Split 6 Defense that has been used by a number of teams for several decades.

The Split 6 Defense utilized eight people on or near the line of scrimmage and would play a three-deep zone secondary. The defensive end away from the flow would work back through the deep third to help on action passes. The end to the side of the action pass would take the flat, and the tackle to his side would contain the quarterback.

The Split 6 Defense was altered by the replacement of the defensive tackles by two linebackers and changes in the technique of the defensive ends. The ends have no pass responsibility in the 80 as they had in the Split 6. The four linebackers and the secondary assumed all the pass responsibility.

The 80 Defense can be shifted into easily from the 50, 40, or 53 Stack Defenses. The offense should be shown a 50, 40, or 53 Stack Defense, and then the 80 should be adopted very smoothly. Again, the defensive signal caller should time the movement so as to keep the quarterback from using his audibles. If a team moves to the 80 from the 53 Stack, the positions that would require movement are the tackles, nose guard, and Willie linebacker. The strong safety and Sam linebacker do not have to shift because they play the same positions and techniques on both defenses. (See Figure 2-16.) The rest of the secondary will adjust to fit the coverage that has been called in the huddle.

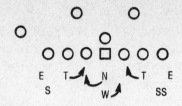

Figure 2-16

The responsibilities of the personnel in the 80 Defense are as follows:

Anchor End—This end should always line up to the left side of the defense regardless of the formation. The anchor plays a 9 technique on the offensive end. In the event of an over-split by the end, the anchor will move down and play a standup 5 technique on the offensive tackle. The anchor end's responsibiliy remains the same on running plays. Against the option, he has the quarterback. On drop back pass plays, he has to contain rush the quarterback. If sprint out action occurs, the anchor end should pull the quarterback up.

Rover End—The rover will have the same responsibilities as the anchor end against both the run and pass. The rover should also be alert for an over-split by the offensive end and be ready to move down to a standup 5 technique.

Left Tackle—Line up in the first defense called in the huddle and be prepared to slide to a 3 technique on the offensive guard. Make a good crisp move and double check your alignment once you reach your final position. Many linemen will not line up properly after they have moved to a new position. Each tackle must realize that in this defense the guard must never reach block the tackle to the inside. If an offensive guard can block the 80 defensive tackle to the inside, the defense is worthless. If the offensive guard releases inside to cut off a scraping linebacker, the tackle must force the guard down at an angle and pursue flat to the line of scrimmage.

Right Tackle—The right tackle will have the same responsibilities as the left tackle. If the offensive guard takes a big split, the tackle will play a head up position and farther off the ball. Where large splits occur frequently, we will gap and stunt the offense with different combinations.

Nose Guard—Move from your original position, whether it be a 0, standup 0, or 2 position, to a standup 1 technique on the guard to the tight end side. If the offense has a two tight end set, go to the formation side guard. On a straight back pass, you will have the near curl or the middle hook, depending on the coverage that has been called. The nose guard should be at a depth from which he can read the release of the near back and the offensive blocking scheme. If the nose guard is involved in a stunt, he should assume the same depth and not tip his intentions. When in the standup 1 technique, the nose guard should realize that the majority of the blocks will come from the offensive tackle if the flow is to his outside. When the flow of the ball is to his inside, the blocks will be by the guard in front of him or the center. He should be prepared to shuffle down the line of scrimmage and shed these blocks.

Sam Linebacker—Sam will move the defense into the 80, based on the quarterback's cadence. He will move to a standup 7 technique on the tight end or the strong side tight end if there is a two tight end formation. Sam must be able to feel the block of the tight end and read the release of the backs. If the end blocks down and the flow is to his outside, Sam must work across the face of the end and keep leverage on the ball. The tight end must never be able to get his head to the inside and turn Sam to the outside. If a drop back pass shows, the Sam linebacker will have the flat. On a sprint out pass, Sam will either cover the near curl or rush. We will build either one of these two options into our game plan, depending on the quarterback, blocking scheme, and pass routes of our upcoming opponent.

Willie Linebacker—This player will move into a standup 1 technique over the inside eye of the guard to the weak side of the formation. Willie and the strong safety will always go the same side of the formation, as do the nose guard and Sam backer. The Willie and the nose guard will have the same basic responsibilities against the running game. Willie must be able to handle the cutback when the flow is away from position. On a drop back pass, he will work the curl that is nearest to his alignment.

Strong Safety—The strong safety must be able to recognize the formation once the offense breaks the huddle. He will go to the split end side even if this side is the strong side. (See Figure 2-17.) If the offense has a closed formation (a two tight end set), the strong safety will go away from the strength of the offense. (See Figure 2-18.) The player in this position must be able to take the pitch on the option to his side and work back through the middle on a flow away from him when we are in 1 Swap coverage. When the strong safety is to be involved in a stunt, he should line up in his normal alignment and slide to the inside at the last moment.

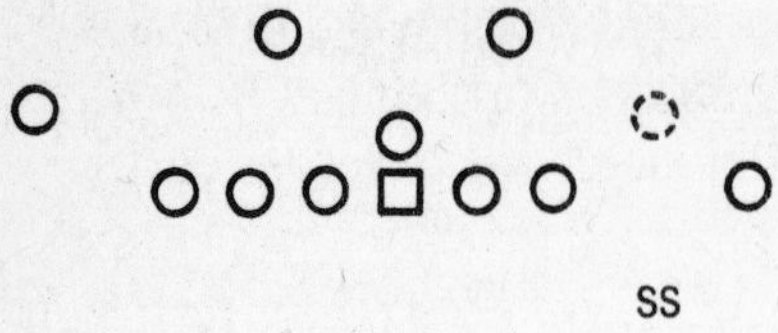

Figure 2-17

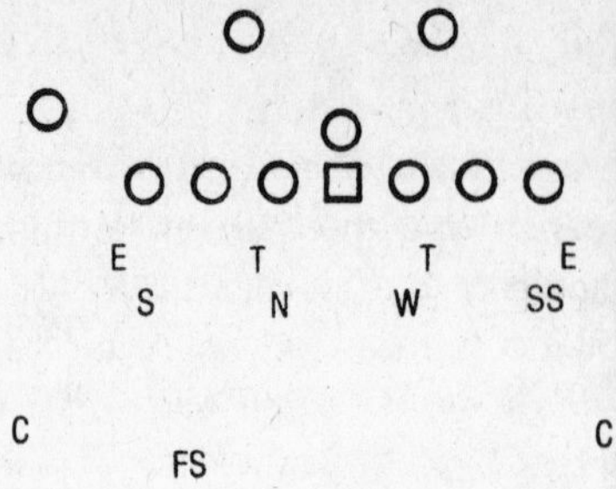

Figure 2-18

Free Safety—The free safety will take his alignment depending upon the formation, coverage, and stunts that are employed in the 80 Defense. The free safety will always go away from the strong safety; hence, he will go always to the tight end side of the offense. If an offense comes out with a two tight end set, we will play man coverage if there are stunts involved in the defensive call. (See Figure 2-19.) If 1 Swap coverage has been called in the huddle and the offense comes out with two tight ends, the free safety will check the coverage to 3 cover. (See Figure 2-20.)

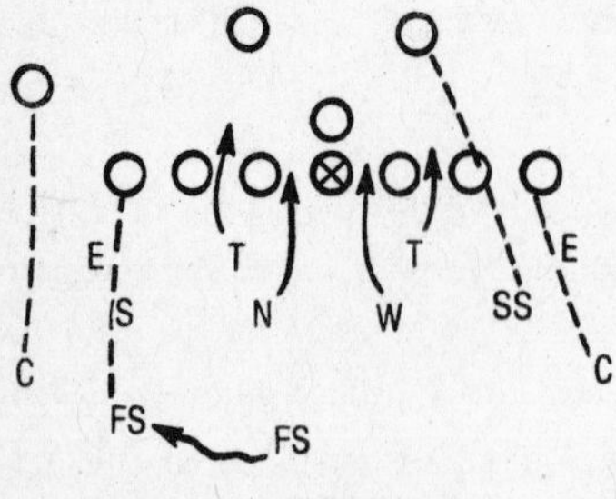

Figure 2-19

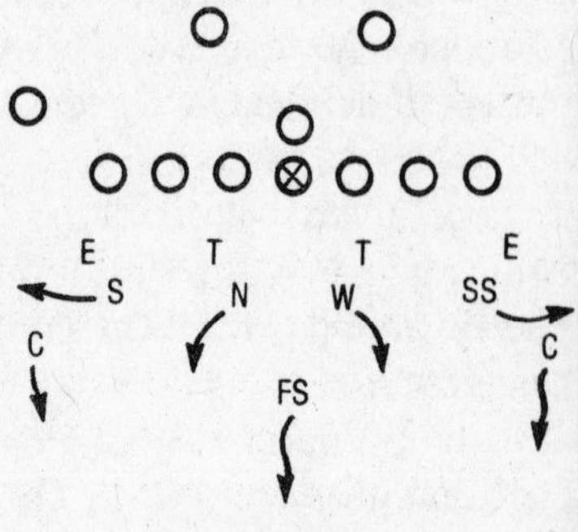

Figure 2-20

Cornerbacks—The corners will take their alignment over the wide outs, as described in chapter 1, if we are playing zone coverage. If man coverage has been called, the corners will take the widest receiver to their side. The defensive back should try to conceal his intent as long as possible, but before the ball is snapped he should be close enough to the receiver to defend against a quick pass.

GOAL LINE DEFENSE

Sometimes it is hard to say what is the most important phase of defensive football. Several coaches say that the third down plays and pass defense are the most important; others say that forcing turnovers is the number one priority; still other coaches maintain that preventing the big play and limiting the offense will win for you. It is my belief that football games are won inside the two ten yard lines on a field. It does not matter how many yards are gained by running or throwing the ball out in the middle of the field; the only important phase of defense is how many points were scored and whether we have more points than our opponents when the final gun sounds. Granted the other objectives are very important, but if a defense is worth its salt, it will force the offense to slow down somewhere on the field. The big plays, of which there will usually be six to eight, generally happen inside the twenty yard stripe on each end of the field. From this line to the goal line is the most important area of defensive football. Remember the first objective listed in this chapter: Don't let our opponents score.

Once the offense gets inside our ten yard line, we must force the issue. Our defense cannot afford to give up yardage while reading the blocking patterns of the offense; we must get penetration by our linemen and frenzied play from the linebackers and secondary. At this point on the field, we emphasize the pride factor, which was last, but not least, on the list of objectives.

Our basic goal line defensive alignment is determined by the offensive sets that we face. We must place our personnel in good positions and teach them the techniques that they need to know in order to get to the ball as quickly as possible. The 60 Defense is shown in Figure 2-21. The majority of adjustments to different formations, motion, and flankers will be made by the secondary and the linebackers. Responsibilities and techniques for each position are as follows:

Ends—The defensive ends must play a 9 technique tight on the offensive end's outside eye, one foot off the ball. At this point on the field, we encourage the ends to play a three-point stance in order to play the drive block more effectively. On the snap of the ball, the end should deliver a blow to the outside shoulder of the tight end. The 9 technique should never allow the offensive end to reach block him. He must come off the block and contain the quarterback if a sweep occurs.

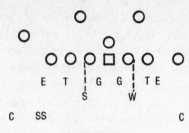

Figure 2-21

Tackles—The defensive tackle's alignment will be head up on the offensive tackle and as tight to the line of scrimmage as possible. On the snap, the defensive player should drive low and hard through the crotch of the offensive tackle. The closer the ball is to the goal line, the lower the tackle will charge. The defensive tackle should aim for a point one yard deep in the opponent's backfield. We want our tackles in a four-point stance inside the four yard line in order to get more thrust and to stay lower.

Guards—The two linemen who are lined up in the 1 techniques between the center and offensive guards must prevent the quarterback sneak. These linemen will line up with their inside feet on each foot of the center. We want these guards to be in a four-point stance, with elbows bent and hips higher than the shoulders. When the ball is snapped, we want these players to explode through the foot of the center with the face bar on the ground. The guard's target is the foot of the quarterback to his side.

Sam Linebacker—This linebacker will be called upon to play in two positions in the 60 Defense. He will play over the center when there is a fullback and over the guard's outside shoulder in a split back formation. When the linebacker is over the center, he will key the quarterback and the ball. The Sam must fill the guard-tackle gap to either side when the ball moves in that direction. If the offense has a split back formation, Sam will key the back in front of him. On a drop back pass, Sam will have the back to his side.

Willie Linebacker—The Willie linebacker will be aligned behind and slightly outside of the defensive tackle to his side when Sam is over the center. When the offense uses a split back formation, Willie should take a position on the outside shoulder of the offensive guard and key the back nearest him. On a drop back pass, Willie has the tailback man for man. On a flow away from him, Willie should work down the line for cutbacks.

Secondary—The play of the secondary on all goal line defenses will be man coverage. We will take one of the safeties out and replace him with a defensive lineman who will play one of the two inside spots. We normally leave our strong safety in the game because of his ability to play the run and take the free safety out.

Strong Safety—Line up on the outside shoulder of the strong side end, two yards deep, and key the block of your man. If he blocks, close just outside of the defensive end and be ready to take on a blocker or tackle the ball carrier. If the end releases, bump him and stay with him.

Cornerbacks—You have man coverage on the widest receiver on your side. If your man is split out, wide align on his inside shoulder at a depth of two yards and don't let him catch the quick pattern to the inside. If the end to your side is tight and blocks down, you must close quickly to the outside of the defensive end and give run support.

GOAL LINE STUNTS

We utilize goal line stunts to force mistakes and create confusion in offensive blocking schemes. We will try to stunt on certain downs and in certain situations. Most teams have a pattern of attack on the goal line that can be established through film breakdowns. Once we think we have this pattern established, it is possible to match the defensive stunts to the goal line offense. For example, if a certain breakdown said that there was a 66 % chance that a certain offense would run between the guards on two and goal from the four yard line, we could use the stunt shown in Figure 2-22.

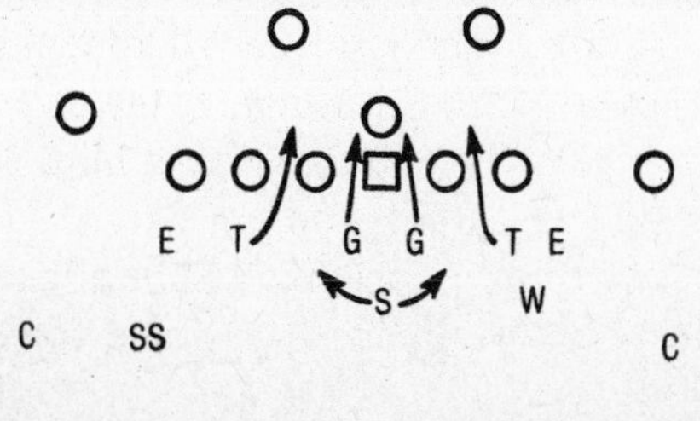

Figure 2-22

The goal line stunts that we will be concerned with in this section will be the 60 Pinch, Slant, and Rush.

60 PINCH

This stunt only concerns the defensive tackles and ends. The other players play their normal 60 techniques. The tackles drive low and hard through the gap between the offensive guard and tackle. This is more of an inside angle than the tackle would normally take on a 60. The defensive ends line up in the regular 60 position, but on the snap of the ball they also drive the gap to their inside, as shown in Figure 2-23.

Figure 2-23

60 SLANT

(See Figure 2-24.) The Slant is a very good call when the offense works to the wide side of the field a great deal and they get on a hash mark. The Slant can be called three different ways: to the strength of the formations, away from the strength, or to the wide side of the field.

Ends—Play your regular 60 techniques.

Tackles—60 alignment. If the Slant is your way, step to the end and then up field; anticipate the end blocking down on you. Don't be reached by the tackle. Stay low.

Guards—If the Slant is coming to your side, cheat to a position

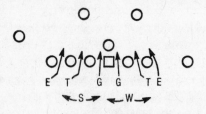

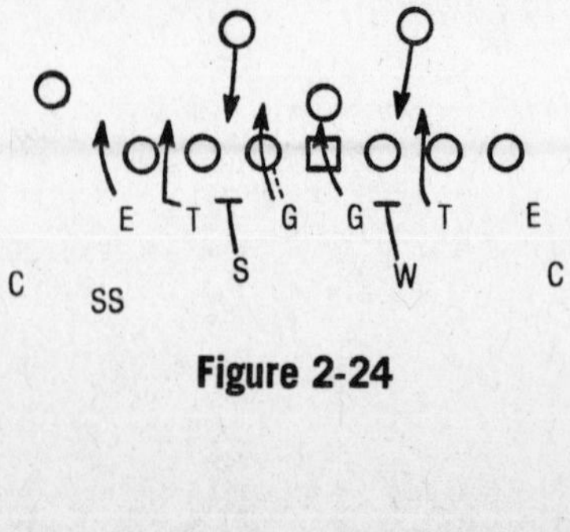

Figure 2-24

over the offensive guard's outside ear. Drive through the guard's outside leg on the snap. If the Slant is away from you, stay in your 60 alignment but drive through the center to the side of the call.

Linebackers—Know the strength of the formation and be ready to either fill or scrape. If the Slant is to you and your near back dives, you must be prepared to fill the gap between your tackle and guard. (See Figure 2-24.) If slant is away from you and the flow is outside you, scrape.

Secondary—The strong safety and cornerbacks play man coverage.

60 RUSH

(See Figure 2-25.) 60 Rush is used to bring a man in every gap on the snap of the ball. Sometimes this is an effective call against a dive play, but I have seen the defender run past the ball carrier. Each man must anticipate a head-on tackle with a back and be prepared to carry him backwards.

Ends—Play the 60 technique, but play it slightly loose. You have the back who flares on your side if a pass play occurs. (See Figure 2-25.)

Tackles—Align in your 60 position. On the snap, excute a slant technique to the outside and contain the quarterback.

Guards—Play a regular 60.

Linebackers—On the snap, fire the gap directly in front of you.

Secondary—You have man coverage.

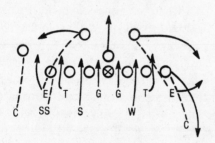

Figure 2-25

CHAPTER 3

HOW TO CONTROL THE VEER OFFENSE
WITH MULTIPLE ALIGNMENTS

The Veer Offense was created a few years ago at the University of Houston. Today, this is one of the most popular offensive series in high school and college football. This offense places tremendous pressure on certain points along the line of scrimmage. This is especially true if you line up in one defense all afternoon.

This is why we believe in multiple defenses. We want to give our opponents the same initial appearance, but just prior to or on the snap of the ball, we will shift our alignment or execute a stunt that will confuse blocking assignments and the quarterback's read.

One of the basic principles in teaching defense is the elimination of mistakes. Even though we believe in multiple alignments, we want the individual techniques to remain as elementary as possible. We feel that by teaching the majority of our defensive personnel two or three techniques we can play any one of the four defenses we utilize against the Veer series. The four alignments that have proven effective for us and a number of teams are the 50, 53 Stack, 70, and the 80 Defenses.

One season the Mississippi State defense was faced with some form of the Veer Offense eight out of twelve games. How well the multiple scheme worked against this type of offense was evidenced by an 8-3 season and a Sun Bowl victory.

The Veer run plays that we will be most concerned with in this chapter will be the inside veer, the outside veer, the counter dive, and the counter option. The passing game is discussed in the latter part of the chapter.

THE 50 AND THE VEER

Even though the Veer Offense was originally designed to be run against the 50, this defensive set remains the most popular. The assignments for the dive, the quarterback, and the pitch are relatively simple, but the techniques must be completely mastered. The 50 Defense has been covered in Chapter 1, but against the Veer the keys for the linebackers will change and the alignment for the tackles and ends will vary slightly.

50

Nose—Play tough 0; read through the center to the quarterback.

Sam—Play a standup 3 technique at three to three and a half yards. Read through the guard to the near back. You must read the release of the back: straight ahead, outside, or away. You must be at a depth from which you can scrape both ways.

Will—Play a standup 3; read the back's release and the guard's block. Be able to scrape both ways. Depth three to three and a half yards.

S.T.—Tough 5; you have dive on the triple option.

W.T.—Tough 5; you have a dive on the triple option. Trail on a flow away.

Anchor—Tough 9; feather the quarterback on the option. (Feathering is the method by which an end slow plays the quarterback.)

Rover—Tough 9; feather the quarterback on the option. If your side is open, play in a drop position. Key the near back and the ball. Check cutback.

S.S.—Play coverage called, usually 1. If the option shows, go through the tight end to the pitch.

S.C.—Play coverage called.

F.S.—Play coverage called unless you check coverage against certain formations.

W.C.—Play coverage called, usually 1.

In the 50 Defense against the base play, the inside veer would be played as shown in Figure 3-1.

The strong tackle must do a good job of keeping the offensive tackle from blocking down on the Sam backer. It is essential that Sam close the seam between the nose guard and the tackle if the ball is given and that Sam also be able to scrape if the ball is pulled. Figure 3-2 shows how the outside veer would be played from the 50.

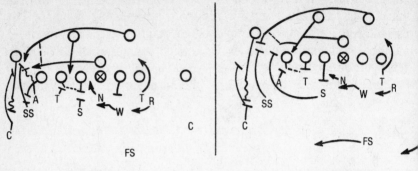

Figure 3-1   **Figure 3-2**

The anchor end now has the same responsibility as the strong tackle did against the inside veer. He must keep Sam free to scrape. After flattening the tight end to the inside, the anchor will take the dive. When the Sam linebacker sees the near back release in the outside veer path, he will scrape to take the quarterback and the strong safety will take the pitch.

The counter dive will be played as shown in Figure 3-3. The depth of the linebackers should be such that they can hang for a fraction of a second to help on the dive and still scrape.

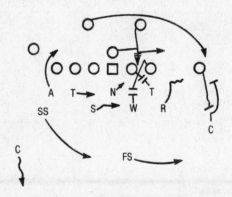

Figure 3-3

The counter option against the 50 would be played as shown in Figure 3-4. The tackle must do a good job of reading the block of the offensive tackle. Some teams will use what we refer to as a sucker block. In a sucker block, the offensive tackle will put his head to the inside to draw you in and then crab you with his legs and hips. You must use your hands to push him down, give some ground, and come off. The end will again use the feather technique on the quarterback, with the cornerback taking the pitch. If the play was run to the strong side, the strong safety would have pitch.

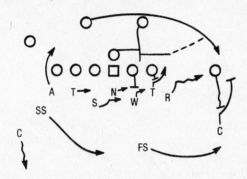

Figure 3-4

STUNTS FROM THE 50 AGAINST THE VEER

The stunts we will use from the 50 are simply an exchange of assignments between two people. We will try to force mistakes by making the quarterback decide quickly whether to give, keep, or pitch. You must work hard at concealing these stunts before the snap or the quarterback will predetermine his option.

BLOOD STUNT (See Figure 3-5)

Our basic play by the defensive ends is to "feather" the quarterback on the option. (The feather technique allows the pursuit to catch up to the ball.) On the Blood Stunt, we want the end to attack the quarterback if the option occurs to his side. The key to this stunt is the release of the tight end. If the tight end releases outside and option action shows, the end attacks the quarterback. If the tight end blocks down, the defensive end closes for the outside veer. If the option is not run, the ends play their normal 9 technique. This stunt only affects the defensive ends. Everyone else plays Base 50. This is an excellent stunt to force bad pitches and to check a quarterback's courage.

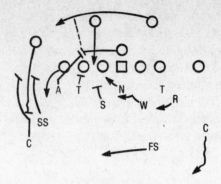

Figure 3-5

PINCH STUNT (See Figure 3-6)

Nose—Play read 0, and do not commit to either side too quickly.

Sam—Apply the Veer key. If the flow is to your side, scrape outside for the quarterback; if the flow is away from you, play 50.

Will—Apply Veer key. If the flow is to your scrape, take the quarterback and play 50.

S.T.—Execute a slant technique to the inside; square shoulders in the hole.

W.T.—Execute a slant technique to the inside.

A—You have the dive. Come down across the face of the tight end to a point directly behind where the offensive tackle lined up.

R—You have the dive. Come across the face of the end if you are playing against a closed formation. If you are playing against an open formation, come down off the tail of the offensive tackle.

S.S.—Play 1 coverage.

S.C.—Play 1 coverage.

F.S.—Play 1 coverage.

W.C.—Play 1 coverage.

The Pinch Stunt is an excellent call on short yardage. It is also very effective on counter dives and counter options when the offensive team is straight blocking.

CROSS STUNT (See Figure 3-7)

Nose—Play tough 0. Get a quick read on the center and go to the ball.

Sam—Apply the Veer key. If the flow is to you, take a short lateral step outside and scrape around your tackle to take the dive; if the flow is away from you, play 50.

Will—Apply the Veer key. If the flow is to you, take a short lateral step outside, scrape around your tackle, and help on the dive; do not run a bow on your scrape; if the flow is away from you, play 50.

S.T.—Execute a slant technique to the inside if the ball is to you. Square your shoulders and do not be driven down. If the flow is away from you, keep coming to the inside.

W.T.—Same as strong tackle.

Anchor—Play 50.

Rover—Play 50. Don't use the drop technique since you must trail on the flow away.

S.S.—Play coverage called.

S.C.—Play coverage called.

F.S.—Play coverage called.

W.C.—Play coverage called.

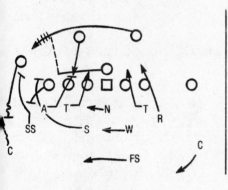

Figure 3-6

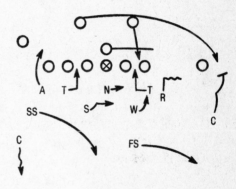

Figure 3-7

BLOOD CROSS (See Figure 3-8)

Nose—Play 0.

Sam—Execute Cross Stunt.

Will—Same as Cross Stunt.

S.T.—Play Cross Stunt.

W.T.—Play Cross Stunt.

Anchor—Play Blood Stunt.

Rover—Play Blood Stunt. You now become the trail man on the flow away.

S.S.—Play coverage.

S.C.—Play coverage.

F.S.—Play coverage.

W.C.—Play coverage.

This is a good change-up stunt that will force the quarterback to make a quick decision. If he decides to pull the ball from the dive, he must pitch exceptionally quickly. Often, the linebacker can scrape all the way to the pitch.

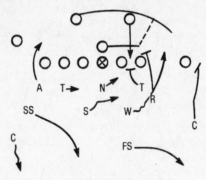

Figure 3-8

X STUNT (Figure 3-9)

Nose—Play 0.

Sam—Play 50; loosen slightly.

Will—Play 50; loosen slightly.

S.T.—Play 50.

W.T.—Execute a slant to the outside: you now have the quarterback and/or contain on a sprint pass.

Anchor—Play 50.

Rover—Play in your normal drop position. If the flow is your way, take a short lateral step to the inside and execute the X Stunt behind your tackle. You now have the dive. If the flow is away from you, work to the inside for cutbacks and counters.

S.S.—Play coverage called.

S.C.—Play coverage called.

F.S.—Play coverage called.

W.C.—Play coverage called.

The X Stunt is probably the best change-up we have to the split end side. The quarterback will read "give" almost every time. The rover end should make the play on the dive for no gain. On the lead option, the rover can come under and take the quarterback, allowing your tackle to come off on the pitch.

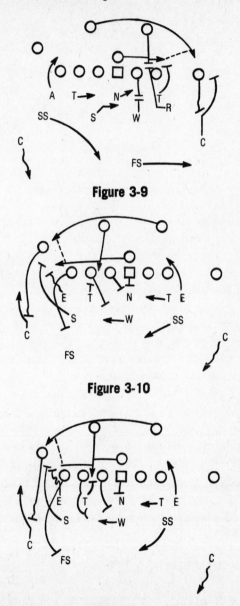

Figure 3-9

Figure 3-10

Figure 3-11

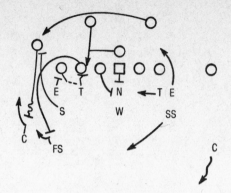

Figure 3-12

THE 53 STACK AND THE VEER

We began experimenting with the 53 Stack as a way of helping us to control the Veer Offense. The result was very gratifying, and we continued to use it with good results. The changes for the defensive positions were minute. We had to teach only three positions—the two linebackers and the strong safety—new techniques.

Basically, we use man coverages against the Veer to take away the Veer pass to the tight end. It is my opinion that this pass is really what makes the Veer so potent.

To be able to defend properly against an offense, you must understand the methods by which the attacking team is trying to move the ball. In Figures 3-10, 3-11, and 3-12, you can readily see that whatever method of blocking is used, the 53 Stack, simply by alignment, can render the Veer ineffective. Against the outside veer with two tight ends, the 53 Stack would be played as shown in Figures 3-13 and 3-14.

The counter option to either side will be played in the same manner as the triple option. The nose guard, Willie, and the tackle at the point of attack have the dive; the end takes the quarterback; and Sam or the strong safety takes the pitch, depending on which side the play is being executed.

The counter dive with fold blocking is the one play that you must work on a great deal. Because of the alignment (the defense is outnumbered five to four), offensive teams try to run between the tackles. We expect our tackles to read the block of the guard, tackle, and limit the gain to two and a half yards. (See Figure 3-15.)

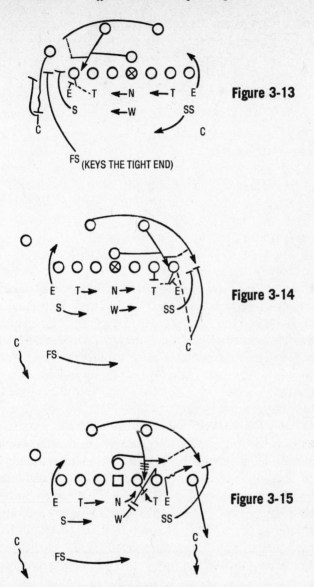

Figure 3-13

FS (KEYS THE TIGHT END)

Figure 3-14

Figure 3-15

VEER STUNTS FROM THE 53 STACK

There are several stunts from the 53 Stack that we feel are excellent change-ups from the normal alignment and will present different reads for the quarterback. These stunts are used to break the rhythm of a drive and to force the offense into a situation that favors the defense. No stunt is ever called unless the type of blocking pattern being used by the offense is known. The stunts are designed to nullify certain patterns, as shown in Figure 3-16.

SWAP STUNT

Nose—Play tough 0.

Sam—53 alignment. If the flow is your way and the tight end releases outside, step up to the inside and take the quarterback quickly on the option. If the flow is away from you, play 53 Stack. If the tight end blocks down, play 53 Stack.

Will—Play 53 Stack.

S.T.—Play Stack.

W.T.—Play Stack.

Anchor—If the flow is to you and the tight end releases outside, take the pitch. If the tight end blocks down, play 53 Stack.

Rover—Play 53 Stack.

S.S.—Man cover.

F.S.—Play slow support on the pitch; check strong receiver for part.

S.C.—Man cover.

W.C.—Man cover.

The Swap Stunt allows us to change-up the assignments on the tight end side and get the Sam backer on the quarterback quickly. Some teams tried to release the tight end around the anchor end and block the scraping linebacker. The release of the offensive end is the key to executing this stunt. If the end does not release around the anchor end, the Swap Stunt is off and we will play our normal techniques on 53 Stack.

RIP STUNT (See Figure 3-17)

Nose—Execute a Dart to the strong side of the formation.

Sam—Play 53 Stack.

Will—Execute a fire technique through the weak side guard-center gap.

S.T.—Play 53 Stack.

W.T.—Play 53 Stack.

Anchor—Play 53 Stack.

Rover—Play 53 Stack.

S.S.—Play man coverage.

S.C.—Play man coverage.

F.S.—Play man coverage.

W.C.—Play man coverage.

The Rip Stunt is a good change-of-pace stunt that is very effective on the counter drive with fold blocking. In man to man coverage, all eligible receivers are covered and you get a maximum pass rush on the quarterback.

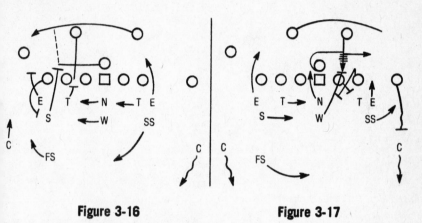

Figure 3-16   **Figure 3-17**

53 STACK RUSH (See Figure 3-18)

Nose—Execute the Rip Stunt.

Sam—Cheat to the inside and slightly deeper than your normal alignment. On the snap of the ball, drive through the guard-tackle gap. Take the dive.

Will—Execute the Rip Stunt.

S.T.—Use a slant technique to the outside. You have a quarterback on the option.

W.T.—Use a slant technique to the outside. You have a quarterback on the option.

Anchor—53 Stack alignment. On an option coming your way, you have the pitch. On a drop back pass, you have the back out of the backfield coming your way.

S.S.—53 Stack alignment. On the snap of the ball, you drive through the guard-tackle gap. Take the dive.

S.C.—4 coverage.

F.S.—4 coverage.

W.C.—4 coverage.

We feel that the 53 Rush is the best in football against the pass. It is well concealed, and the backs can release in only one direction on a drop back pass: in a flare pattern. If you combine this rush with the 53 Prevent, which will be discussed in a later chapter, the quarterback cannot read your defense.

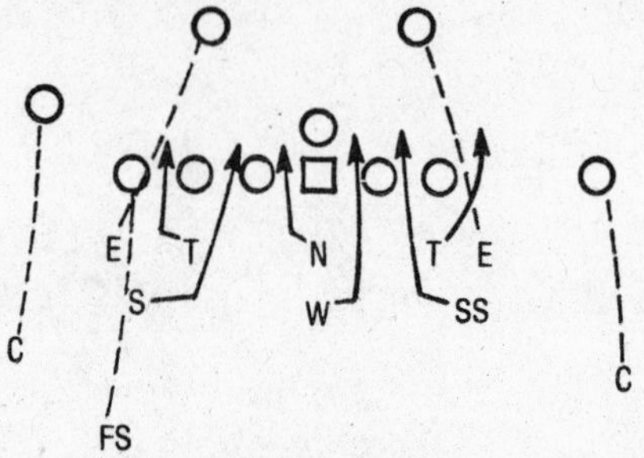

Figure 3-18

70 DEFENSE

The 70 Defense is a combination defense. It is a combination of the 50 Defense and the 80 Defense, which will be discussed later in this chapter. The 70 Defense is extremely good against a split end formation. If we faced a team that featured a closed formation, we would probably not include the 70 in our game plan or we would check this call on the line of scrimmage. The 70 Defense against the inside veer would be defended as shown in Figure 3-19.

On a flow away, the rover end now must have trail responsibility since the weak tackle is working down inside. (See Figure 3-19.) On the option to the weak side, the tackle and Willie must take the dive, and the rover still feathers the quarterback.

The counter option would be handled in much the same manner as the inside veer. The inside people have the dive, the ends have the quarterback, and the secondary handles the pitch.

In Figure 3-20, we illustrate how the outside veer should be played from the 70 Defense. Sam's assignment is the same in the 70 as it is in Base 50. Sometimes the tight end will try to combo block with the offensive tackle. When we discover this, we will run our Bingo

Slant to him, and he now has to stay with the 5 technique or the tackle will take the dive.

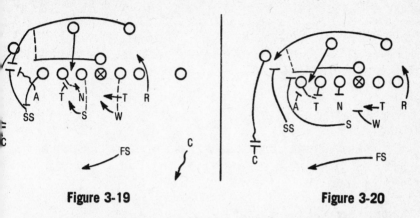

Figure 3-19   **Figure 3-20**

The counter dive to the weak side with a fold block would be layed as shown in Figure 3-21. The linebackers overlap in the middle. Willie must not run himself out of the play too quickly. Sam and the ose guard squeeze from the backside.

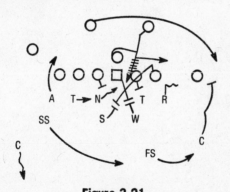

Figure 3-21

BASIC 70 STUNTS

The basic 70 stunts are well concealed, and the position techniques were learned for the Base 50, although three new terms must be learned. The first stunt we teach in 70 is the Dart Stunt. The stunt is called both to the strength and weakness of the formation. The 70 Strong Dart is shown in Figure 3-22.

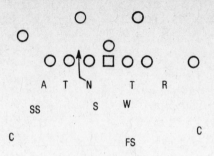

Figure 3-22

The only position that the Dart Stunt will affect is the Sam backer. Sam must know which gap will be taken by the nose guard and compensate for it.

BINGO SLANT (See Figure 3-23)

Nose—70 alignment. Execute a Strong Dart.

Sam—Hang longer inside because your nose guard is slanting out. If a drop back pass occurs, work the strong curl.

Will—Play 70. On a drop back pass, work the backside curl.

S.T.—Line up in a loose 5 technique, execute a slant to the outside, and pull up the quarterback on sprint pass. Take the quarterback on the inside veer.

W.T.—Play a 3 technique.

Anchor—Play your regular 9 technique.

Rover—Play a standup 5 technique.

S.S.—Play coverage called.

S.C.—Play coverage called.

F.S.—Play coverage called.

W.C.—Play coverage called.

OSKIE SLANT (See Figure 3-24)

Nose—70 alignment. Execute a Weak Dart.

Sam—Play 70. Know that your nose guard is going weak side.

Will—70 alignment. Hang inside slightly longer than usual because your tackle is slanting outside.

S.T.—Play 70.

W.T.—Execute a slant to the outside.

Anchor—Play 70.

Rover—Play 70.
S.S.—Play coverage called.
F.S.—Play coverage called.
S.C.—Play coverage called.
W.C.—Play coverage called.

The Oskie Slant is helpful to the 70 Defense because it balances the defense. The defense has overloaded the formation to the strong side. Against the counter option, the tackle can sometimes take the quarterback if the guard tries to reach and block him. (See Figure 3-25.)

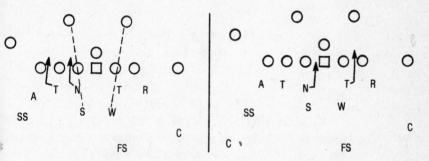

Figure 3-23   **Figure 3-24**

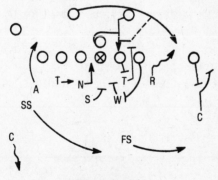

Figure 3-25

THE 80 DEFENSE

The 80 Defense is excellent against the Veer because it does not give the quarterback a true read on the dive. The quarterback is taught to read the first man to the outside of the offensive tackle. In the 80, the first man to the outside of the tackle is not responsible for the dive. The 80 is designed to have the inside linebacker and 3 technique take the dive. The ends have the quarterback; and the strong safety or the Sam backer have the pitch.

The majority of the techniques up front have been previously learned in the other defenses. The tackles know the 3 technique from playing the 70, the ends have a regular 9 technique, Sam plays the 53 Stack position, and Willie plays the 70 technique. The secondary plays the same zone coverage as in Base 50, but the positions of the strong safety and the free safety have been reversed against a pro formation. The only position that requires teaching time is the nose guard, who now becomes a linebacker.

The advantages of the 80 Defense is that it is an exceptional run defense, with eight people that can give quick run support. A team is also capable of playing the stack look in the middle against a closed formation, and the 80 is a good stunting defense. The inside veer against the 80 Defense would be played as shown in Figure 3-26.

The outside veer would be played as shown in Figures 3-27 and 3-28. The strong safety would go to the weak side of the formation against two tight ends and take the quarterback exactly as in the 53 Stack. The secondary should be in man coverage.

The counter option would be played the same way as the inside veer, with the four inside people responsible for the dive, the ends responsible for the quarterback, and the strong safety and Sam on the pitch. In the zone coverage that we employ, the defense can get an additional man on the pitch to the strong side.

The counter dive must be taken by the four inside people. The

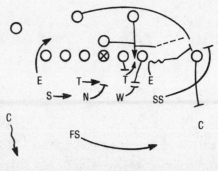

Figure 3-26

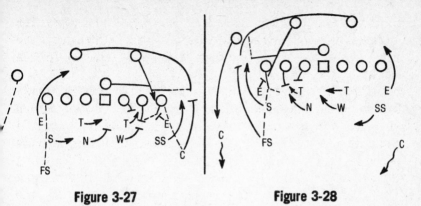

Figure 3-27   **Figure 3-28**

tackles must squeeze from the outside and the linebackers overlap. The nose guard and Willie must hang inside anytime the quarterback spins. Their depth should be such that they can let the back break inside or outside of the 3 technique and they can make the tackle.

VEER STUNTS FROM THE 80

80 SWAP (See Figure 3-29)

Nose—Play 80. If a drop back pass occurs, you have curl to your side.

Sam—Play the 53 Stack Swap. If the tight end releases outside the anchor end and the option shows, you have the quarterback. If the tight end blocks down, you play 80.

Will—Play 80.

S.T.—Play 80.

W.T.—Play 80.

Anchor—Play the 53 Stack Swap. If the tight end releases around you and the option shows, take the pitch. If anything else shows, play 80.

Rover—On open formations play 80. On a two tight-end set, if the end releases around you and the option shows, take the pitch. If the end blocks down, you play 80.

Strong Safety—Play coverage called versus open sets. Against a two tight end formation, if the end releases outside the rover and the option shows, take the quarterback quickly.

S.C.—Play coverage called.

F.S.—Play coverage called.

W.C.—Play coverage called.

A number of teams will release the end around the defensive end and try to pick off the scraping linebacker. When this scheme is shown, we will call the Swap Stunt. If the ball is not given on the dive, the quarterback must pitch very quickly.

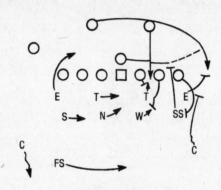

Figure 3-29

80 OUT (See Figure 3-30)

Nose—80 alignment. Hang inside longer because your tackle is slanting outside. Read the path of the back on the dive.

Sam—Play 80.

Will—80 alignment. Hang inside longer because your tackle is going outside. Read the backs on the dive.

S.T.—Execute an outside technique; step laterally with the outside foot, anticipating the offensive tackle to block down. If the ball is coming outside you, square your shoulders and come upfield. If the ball is going away from you, run behind the offensive guard.

W.T.—Execute the Out technique; same as the strong tackle.

Anchor—Play 80.

Rover—Play 80.

S.S.—Play coverage called.

S.C.—Play coverage called.

F.S.—Play coverage called.

W.C.—Play coverage called.

The 80 Out is a call that is used to force the offensive tackle to double team the 3 technique on the inside veer. This stunt allows your linebackers a certain amount of freedom since the offensive tackle cannot come off the 3 technique to pick off the scraping linebacker.

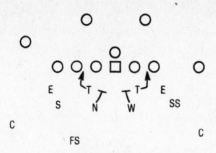

Figure 3-30

80 SLANT STRONG (See Figure 3-31)

Nose—80 alignment. Know which way your tackle is slanting. Have proper depth to scrape. Key the near back.

Sam—Play 80.

Will—80 alignment. Know the direction of the slant, have proper depth, and key near the back.

S.T.—80 alignment. Listen to the linebacker call to determine which way to slant. On the snap of the ball, either go inside or outside the guard.

W.T.—Same as S.T.

Anchor—Play 80.

Rover—Play 80.

S.S.—Play coverage called.

S.C.—Play coverage called.

F.S.—Play coverage called.

W.C.—Play coverage called.

The 80 Slant Strong (Weak) is one of the most distracting stunts from this defense. It is called depending on the offensive tendencies and situations.

80 RUSH (See Figure 3-32)

Nose—80 alignment. On the snap, drive through the guard-center gap.

Sam—80 alignment. On the snap, drive through the end-tackle gap.

Will—80 alignment. On the snap, drive through the guard-center gap.

S.T.—On the snap, drive through the guard-tackle gap.

W.T.—On the snap, drive through the guard-tackle gap.

Anchor—Check for a dump pass to the third receiver to your side. If there is no third receiver to your side, rush.

Rover—Rush, unless two tight ends or the third receiver are to your side.

Strong Safety—Against two tight ends, fire the end-tackle gap. Against a split end team, you have the second eligible receiver to your side.

S.C.—Man coverage.

F.S.—Man coverage. You have the second eligible receiver to your side.

W.C.—Man coverage.

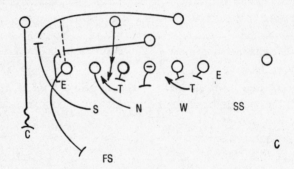

Figure 3-31

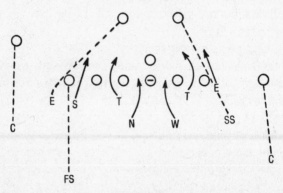

Figure 3-32

SECONDARY COVERAGES AGAINST THE VEER

In modern football, the defensive secondary positions are the most challenging spots for an athlete. In a very few seconds, a long pass can put points on the scoreboard. The secondary must be able to cover the receivers and still support on the running game.

The Veer Offense has put more pressure than ever on the defensive backfield. For a split second after the ball is snapped, the secondary does not know if the play is run or pass.

Secondary calls are coordinated with the call made for the front seven. This is a must in order to have a good, overall, balanced defense. The two schemes we play in the secondary are man coverage, used on the rushes and the 53 Stack, and zone coverage, used on all other calls.

Some of the techniques for the secondary positions have been discussed elsewhere. We will be concerned with fitting the coverages to the defensive fronts.

1 coverage can be played with all 50 and 70 calls, although in most 70 calls the linebackers must understand that they have the curl zones because the rover is committed to the rush. This coverage is the basic coverage and must be learned well. On a drop back pass, the corners and the free safety have the deep thirds; Sam has the strong curl, Willie works the weak side curl, and the rover works the curl and breaks to the flat.

On a run to the strong side, the strong safety has run support and the corners and free safety play the thirds. When the run shows to the weak side, the weak corner supports and the free safety works the outside third. The strong safety must work the deep middle, and the strong corner must work the deep third.

A good change-up against a Veer team is to have the free safety support on the run and the weak corner play the deep third. This 1 invert to the weak side will confuse the blocking pattern of the split end. (See Figure 3-33.)

1 Swap is played in conjunction with the 80 Defense and the 53 Stack Defense. The responsibilities are the same as in 1 coverage, but the positions of the strong safety and the free safety are reversed.

The 2 Call can be played with any 40, 50, 70, or 80 Defense. The cornerbacks should force the wide receivers to the inside and alter the routes as much as possible. The strong safety and the free safety play the deep halves. The corners have the pitch on the option, the flat on a drop back pass, and option passes. This is an excellent call against a quick out pattern. This coverage is played regardless of the flow of the ball.

Cover 2 Roll is played the same as the 2 Call if the ball goes straight back. If the ball goes to either side of the formation, the secondary will revolve in the direction of the flow. Cover 2 Roll can also be played with any 40, 50, 70, or 80 Defense.

Cover 3 is played in conjunction with Base 50 or 40 Defense, with only a short time before half time or the end of a game. The corners are responsible for their respective thirds, the free safety has the middle third, and the strong safety has the flat to his side. If option action develops to the strong side of the formation, the free safety must try to recover and help as much as possible on the tight end pass.

Cover 4-Reverse is played when the 80 Rush or 53 Stack Rush is called. The corners have the wide receivers, and the free safety has the second eligible receiver to the strong side. The strong safety will either rush or have the back to his side. One of the ends will be responsible for picking up the remaining back.

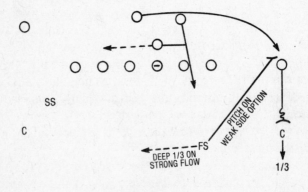

1 INVERT

Figure 3-33

CHAPTER 4

DEFENDING AGAINST
THE WISHBONE OFFENSE

In the early 40's, a new offense came on the college football scene. This innovative formation was called the Split T because of the wide offensive line spacings. In this offense, the plays that were so effective were the quick hitting dive plays and the quarterback option. All of these plays, the dive, fullback off tackle, and option, were run in sequence, thus giving the defense the same initial look in the early stages of each play.

The Wishbone Offense that is so popular in high school and college football today is basically the Split T with certain modifications. For a team to be able to defend against a particular formation, they must first understand the offensive philosophy and the strongest attacking points of the formation. There are a number of plays that Wishbone teams can and do use, but we will be referring to the features plays that make this formation so effective. These plays are shown in Figures 4-1 through 4-6.

After studying the strengths of the Wishbone, we felt we must be able to do certain things to defend properly against this formation. First, we must be in a balanced defense and have definite responsibilities for the dive, quarterback, and pitch. We want these responsibilities to remain as constant as possible, even though we may be in different fronts.

Second, we must have good pass coverage against the favorite routes of our opponents and still be able to support the run game with our secondary. The defensive backfield must get a correct read on the quarterback and tell by his third step if the play is to be a pass or run.

Third, the defense must present different defensive looks and change-ups in order to prevent a constant read by the quarterback. These looks also force a change in blocking patterns at the last instant, and sometimes a missed assignment by an offensive lineman can result in a big play for the defense. Early in the second quarter of a Mississippi State vs. Alabama game, we moved our defense from the 50 to the 70 Defense and ran an Oskie Slant. Our fine nose guard, Harvey Hull, intercepted a pitchout and ran thirty-five yards for a touchdown to tie the game at that point.

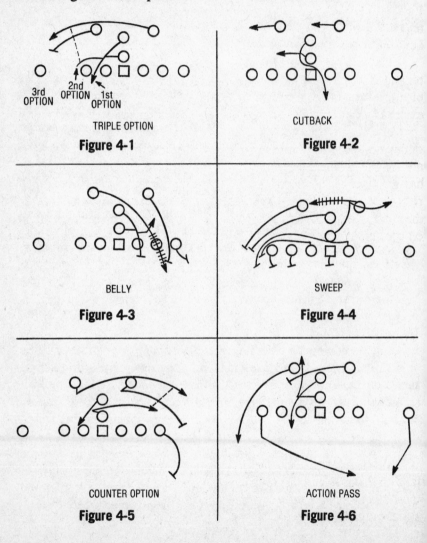

TRIPLE OPTION

Figure 4-1

CUTBACK

Figure 4-2

BELLY

Figure 4-3

SWEEP

Figure 4-4

COUNTER OPTION

Figure 4-5

ACTION PASS

Figure 4-6

THE 50 AND THE WISHBONE

We feel that the 50 Defense with the four-spoke secondary is an excellent defense against the Wishbone formation for two main reasons. First, the defense is balanced and we can easily stunt any of the front seven people. Second, we can change-up the responsibilities for the quarterback and the pitch with the secondary and ends. We feel this ability to change-up is a must in order to slow down the Wishbone.

The techniques of the 50 Defense have been discussed in Chapter 1 and will not be reviewed here. There will not be a change in the basic techniques of the linemen and the secondary. There will be a change in keys for the linebackers. They must key the near back and the fullback.

We will take the plays that were diagrammed earlier in this chapter and show how the 50 Defense will be played. There will be various blocking schemes that may change the play of a position to a small extent from week to week, but the basic plays must be mastered.

The first and most basic play that we must control is the triple option or inside veer. The nose guard, the tackle, and the linebacker are assigned to the dive; the end has the quarterback; and the secondary has the pitch. (See Figure 4-7.) The defensive end should read the release of the near back to tell if the onside back is blocking on him or the corner. If the back is blocking on him, he must still keep leverage on quarterback, use his hands to shed the blocker, and tackle.

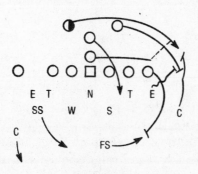

Figure 4-7

When the cutback play is run against the 50, the responsibility falls on the nose guard, the linebacker, and the tackle. The nose guard must be in a tight 0 and keep leverage on the ball; the linebacker must key the fullback and the near back. If both players go away and the guard fires straight out, he must step up and close the seam between himself and the nose-guard. The defensive tackle must work across the face of the offensive tackle to close from the outside.

When defending against the inside belly play, we must get good technique play from the linebacker, tackle, and end. The defensive end must work back across the face of the tight end once he recognizes a turn-out block. The defensive tackle should jam the offensive tackle and force him to release flat down the line, and take the dive by the fullback. The linebacker should be aware of the release of the near back. When he sees the back diving toward him, the linebacker should be prepared to scrape around his tackle and take on this blocker. (See Figure 4-8.)

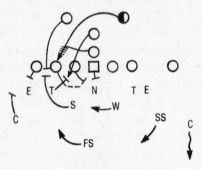

Figure 4-8

Against the sweep, the secondary must turn the play to the inside as the end and the tackle defeat the reach block and react to the ball. The linebackers should read full flow by all backs and scrape outside.

Against the counter option, the linemen must read the blocks by the offensive line and come off to the correct pursuit lane. The defensive end should slam the tight end who is releasing and take the quarterback. The linebackers should hang when the backs take a counter step and the quarterback spins. Both backers must recognize the play, keep leverage on the ball, and overlap all areas. The secondary must rotate and take the pitch.

Passes from the Wishbone are sometimes difficult to cover, because the majority of passes come off a run play fake. The secondary and underneath people need a lot of work to recognize these patterns quickly. We would play our basic coverage from the 50 Defense, which would be 1 coverage.

WISHBONE STUNTS FROM THE 50

X STUNT (See Chapter 3)

The X Stunt is a change-up that gives the quarterback a "give" read on the tackle. The defensive end must come farther inside to take the fullback dive against the Wishbone than he would if the offense was in a pro formation.

50 EAGLE (See Figure 4-9)

The Eagle against the Wishbone is not really a stunt, but an adjustment that will help on the fullback cutback to the split end side. This alignment will also give the quarterback problems on the first read to the split end side because he now must make a decision on whether to read the end or Willie linebacker.

Anchor—Play 50.

Rover—Slide down and play a standup 5 technique. On a flow away, you are to trail two feet outside of the tackle to the split end side.

S.T.—Play 50.

W.T.—Play a 3 technique on the guard.

Nose—Play a tough 0.

Sam—Play 50.

Willie—Play a standup 5 as you would in the 40.

Secondary—Play 1 coverage.

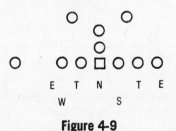

Figure 4-9

50 STRONG SLANT STAY (See Figure 4-10)

The Strong Slant Stay call can be run either to the weak or strong side. We will only discuss one way: to the strength of the formation. This call can be effective on counter plays, and it can allow your linebackers to scrape quickly on a flow.

Anchor End—Play 50.

Rover End—You have no pass responsibility. On a flow away, trail behind the line as deep as the ball.

S.T.—Play 50.

W.T.—On the snap, beat the offensive tackle to the inside gap. If the flow is to you, take the fullback. On a flow away, close down looking for a cutback.

Nose—Execute a Strong Dart.

Sam—Loosen up slightly and be ready to scrape behind the nose guard on a flow to the weak side. Same keys as in 50.

Will—Play the same keys as in 50, but realize you have help in the guard-tackle gap. On a strong flow, be ready to fill the area between you and the nose guard. On a weak flow, be ready to scrape outside the slant tackle.

Secondary—Play 1 coverage.

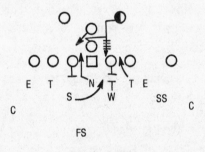

Figure 4-10

50 WHAM (See Figure 4-11)

The Wham stunt is another change-up that helps our defense confuse the blocking scheme of the Wishbone. When the lead halfback is blocking on either the end or a secondary man, changing our responsibilities at the last instant gives us the edge. We will only run this call to the split end side.

Anchor—Play 50.

Rover—Align as in 50. If the option shows your way, begin to widen slightly as you normally do, but after three to four steps get up field quickly and take the pitch. If the option does not occur, play 50.

S.T.—Play 50.

W.T.—Play 50.

Nose—Play 50.

Sam—Play 50.

Will—Play 50.

Corners—Play 50.

F.S.—Play 50.

S.S.—Align to the split end of the formation and key the quarterback. If option action shows to your side, squat and come underneath the end to take the quarterback if he continues down the line. If the quarterback fakes to the fullback and drops back, you should backpedal and check for the onside back flaring.

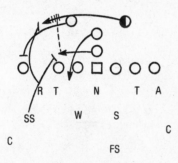

Figure 4-11

THE 53 STACK AND THE WISHBONE (See Figure 4-12)

This defense is useful against the Wishbone since it allows an overload to the tight end side. This overload can be very helpful if a team has a tendency to run the option, the belly play, or the sweep to the tight end side. The defense has been stretched to help on the outside so the tackles, Willie linebacker, and nose guard must do a good job on the inside.

We will show how the 53 Stack should be played against the basic plays in the Wishbone. The defense should be used as a change of pace and according to the situation.

Against the inside veer or triple option, the linebackers, nose guard, and tackles must take care of the dive by the fullback. The Sam linebacker, even though he is outside the strong tackle, must hang inside to help on the dive. Sam must be ready to take the fullback if the defensive tackle gets blocked down. (See Figure 4-12.) Sam must learn that he is to scrape for the pitch when the secondary is in man coverage and hang for the dive in zone coverage. In zone coverage, the corner will take the pitch.

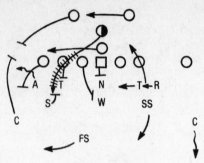

Figure 4-12

To defend against the cutback play by the fullback, a great job must be done by the tackles. They must close the seam between where they are lined up and the nose guard. We put the tackles in a 4 technique when facing the Wishbone so that they have a better chance of closing the cutback lane. The nose guard should play a tough 0 in order to help on this play. Sam should be able to give some help if the cutback is run to the tight end side, and the slants that will be discussed later should help to the split end side.

The inside belly play which is a favorite of all teams, should not present a problem to the 53 Stack because your Sam linebacker is in a good position to make the play. In the 50 Defense, when the backer read the belly play, he scraped to the position that he has now assumed. The tackle, the nose guard, and Willie must take the threat of the fullback; the anchor end and Sam must close the hole between the tight end and offensive tackle.

The sweep to the tight end side should not be that much of a problem. If the tight end blocks out on the defensive end, the Sam backer can come up field and cause a lot of confusion. If both guards pull and the offensive tackle blocks on the 4 technique, the Willie linebacker can run through the onside gap. (See Figure 4-13.)

Stunts from the 53 Stack that are used against the Wishbone will be to give the quarterback a difficult read and to force the quarterback to make very quick decisions and, we hope, a bad decision. As always, the blocking scheme of the offense will dictate what stunts a defense can run. The stunts from the 53 Stack that are basic for us against this formation are the Swap, Dart, and Slant.

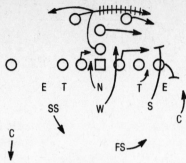

Figure 4-13

SWAP (See Figure 4-14)

Anchor—Play a 9 technique, realizing that if the option shows your way the Sam linebacker will jump the quarterback quickly. You can be conscious of helping on the pitch man, with the quarterback taken by Sam. If you do not get the option, play your regular 9 technique.

Rover—Play a 9 technique as described for the anchor if you have the Sam linebacker to your side.

S.T.—Play a 4 technique.

W.T.—Play a 4 technique.

Sam—Play a standup 7 technique and read the ball. If you feel the tight end releasing outside and option shows to your side, you must step up and take the quarterback immediately. If no option occurs, play your normal 7 technique.

Willie—Play the standup 0 behind the nose guard and key the flow.

Secondary—Play 1 coverage.

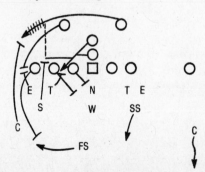

Figure 4-14

The Swap stunt is an excellent call against the option to the tight end side. If the onside halfback is blocking on the end to free the quarterback, you still have someone assigned to the quarterback. If the halfback is blocking on the corner, the end is free to help on the pitch.

53 STACK DART

The Dart is a basic stunt that is always carried in the 53 Stack. We feel that the nose guard can cause a lot of problems for the offense if the Dart is used quite a bit. The offense cannot afford to double team the nose guard because this will free the Willie linebacker. The Dart was discussed in Chapter 3.

53 STACK SLANT (See Figure 4-15)

The 53 Stack Slant is one of the best stunts against the Wishbone. As was said earlier, the 53 Stack is overloaded to the tight end side, but the Slant will balance the defense. To the split end side, there is a change of assignments between the end and the tackle that should present a problem to the quarterback on his read. If the option is run to the tight end side, the Sam backer should help on the dive. The Slant will always be run to the split end side of the formation. If two tight ends are used, the Slant will be checked and the secondary will play three deep, with the onside corner taking the pitch and the free safety and the backside corner taking the deep halves of the field.

Anchor—Play a 9 technique. If your side has a split end, you must execute an X-Go with your tackle. You must go through the hip of the offensive tackle straight for the fullback. You must move on the snap and stay as tight to the line of scrimmage as possible. If the flow starts away from you, stay close to the line of scrimmage and look for the cutback by the fullback.

Rover—Play a 9 technique. If you have the split end to your side, play the stunt as described for the anchor end.

Strong Tackle—Align in a 4 technique. On the snap, drive hard through the guard-tackle gap, looking for the fullback. If the flow goes away from you, the tackle should continue down the line, looking for the ball breaking back.

Weak Tackle—Line up in a 5 technique and make sure you can avoid the reach block by the tackle. On the snap, step to the outside and be ready to take the quarterback on the option. If the flow goes away from you, you must trail as deep as the ball, looking for reverses and bootlegs.

Nose—Execute a Dart to the split end side of the formation.

Sam—Play a 7 technique, but on the snap take a step to the inside and look for the fullback.

Willie—Play your normal 53 alignment.

Secondary—Play 1 coverage. If there are two tight ends, the free safety will check the coverage to 3 level.

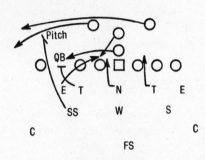

Figure 4-15

THE 70 DEFENSE VERSUS THE WISHBONE (See Figure 4-16)

The 70 Defense is very good against the Wishbone because it overloads the formation to the tight end side. The 70 will also make the offense cut down on line splits, and it is an excellent stunting alignment. The responsibilities for each position against the triple option remain the same as in the 50 Defense, with the nose guard, linebackers, and tackles having the dive, the ends on the quarterback, and the secondary taking the pitch.

When the option is run to the split-end side, the tackle must not be reached by the guard, he must help take the dive. Willie must stay in an inside-out position on the fullback, and if the fullback breaks outside of his guard, he must take a lateral step, square up, and make the tackle.

When the belly play is run to the tight end side, the offense must make a decision whether to block down or out with the tackle to the tight end side. If the tackle turns out on the 5 technique, the Sam is free to fill wherever the back breaks. If the tackle blocks down, the 5 technique must keep the linebacker free to scrape to the ball.

The cutback play must be stopped by the inside linebackers, nose guard, and tackle. The nose guard must play head up on the guard and work to the inside once he recognizes the offensive lineman's block.

When the offense uses the counter option play a great deal, the 70 should be as good a defense as a team can use. The linebackers should keep leverage on the ball as they work inside out. The ends will slow play the quarterback and sprint to close the running lane as the secondary forces the pitchman to the inside.

The sweep should be turned to the inside by the corner as the inside people come off the reach blocks. The correct pursuit angles must be taken as quickly as possible, because the success of a sweep play depends upon the blockers creating a gap between the defensive personnel.

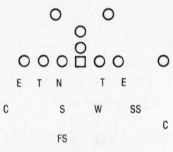

Figure 4-16

70 BINGO SLANT (See Figure 4-17)

Whenever a stunt is incorporated into a defensive scheme, there must be very good reasons, and usually the blocking patterns of the opponents will determine this. The Bingo Slant was put into our package in order to help our defense against the different blocking schemes to the tight end side. Against the play shown in Figure 4-17, if the offensive tackle blocks down on the nose guard, the 5 technique and Sam are free. If the tackle blocks down on Sam, the nose guard and defensive tackle should be at the point of attack. Against the triple option, the nose guard and Sam take the dive by the fullback, and the tackle can jump the quarterback quickly in order to alleviate pressure on the defensive end if the near back is load blocking him.

The responsibilities and coaching points for each position are as follows:

Anchor—Play a 9 technique. Realize that the slant will be coming to your side and loosen slightly.

Rover—Play a standup 5 technique. The slant does not affect you.

Strong Tackle—Line up in a 5 technique and execute a slant to the tight end, reading the tackle as you step. If the offensive tackle blocks down, you must close back to the inside, looking for the lead back coming on you in the belly play or the quarterback on the option.

Nose—Align in a 2 technique on the strong side guard. On the snap, execute a dart to the strong side, reading the block of the guard. If the guard is reaching you, beat him and look for the ball. If the guard is blocking away, run around and work flat to the line as you pursue.

Weak Tackle—Play a 3 technique.

Sam—Play a standup 1 and hang inside with the ball as long as it remains inside the nose guard. When the ball moves outside of the offensive guard tackle gap, you should begin to scrape down the line, still maintaining an inside-outside position on the ball.

Willie—Play a standup 1 technique to the split end side. On a flow to the tight end side, work the middle for the cutback. On a flow to you, take the dive by the fullback.

Defensive Backfield—The secondary can play 1 or 2 coverage.

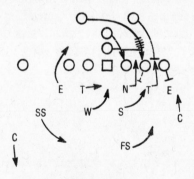

Figure 4-17

OSKIE SLANT (See Figure 4-18)

The Oskie Slant will only concern the nose guard, the weak tackle, and the two linebackers. This stunt helps our defense to the split end side since most teams prefer to run away from the overload to the tight end side. The cutback by the fullback is taken away, and the nose guard can free the Sam linebacker to go to the ball. The defensive tackle to the split end side can force a double team from the offensive guard and tackle on the triple option, and this frees Willie to take the dive by the fullback. (See Figure 4-18.)

Coaching points for the Oskie are explained as follows:

Anchor—Play a 9 technique.

Rover—Play a standup 5 technique.

Strong Tackle—Play a regular 5 technique.

Weak Tackle—Align in a 3 technique. On the snap, step to the offensive tackle and read the block of the guard. Anticipate the tackle blocking down on you and stay low. If the flow is away from you, run around the guard and pursue.

Nose—Line up in a 2 technique and dart to the split end side, looking for the fullback. If you are darting into the flow of the ball stay tight to the line of scrimmage. If you dart away from the flow, run around the guard and get into the correct pursuit lane.

Sam—This linebacker must be aware of where the seams in the slant will develop. He should hang inside and protect against counters and cutbacks in case the nose guard gets turned down the line of scrimmage and the back hits the area between the nose guard and strong tackle.

Willie—Play a standup 1 technique. You must be aware that your tackle is slanting to the outside. Position yourself at a depth at which you can step inside or outside and take the fullback on the dive. Willie should never scrape outside so fast that he allows the fullback to hit between the 3 technique and himself.

Secondary—Play 1 or 2 coverage.

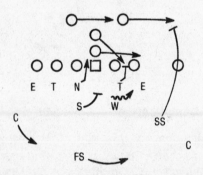

Figure 4-18

THE 70 WIDE (See Figure 4-19)

This alignment is used to change responsibilities against the triple option to the tight end side and to get extra support from the secondary to the split end side. The 70 Defense that was explained earlier in this chapter and the 70 Wide are basically the same, with one exception: The tackle to the strongside lines up on the inside shoulder of the tight end instead of playing a 5 technique on the tackle.

We will play the 70 Wide with the same assignments as in the 70. The tackles, nose guard and the two inside linebackers have the dive by the fullback plus all cutbacks and counter plays. There is only one adjustment made that is different from the 70 Defense. The tackle to the strong side must come down hard through where the offensive tackle lined up to help on the dive. His angle must be through the inside foot of the offensive tackle as shown in Figure 4-19. The secondary can play either 1 or 2 coverage, usually 1.

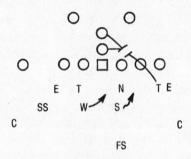

E   T   N   T E

SS   W   S

C   C

FS

Figure 4-19

70 WIDE-GO (See Figure 4-20)

The key to using the 70 Wide alignment is playing what we call 70 Wide-Go. This change of assignments will help a defense conceal who has the dive, quarterback, and pitch. The 70 Wide-Go should also be of value against the belly play and triple option series to the split end side of formation.

Anchor—Line up in a loose 9 technique. On the snap of the ball, take a lateral step with the outside foot in order to make sure you are not reached by the tight end. If the tight releases outside and the option shows, you take the pitch. If the tight end blocks out on you, work back across his face.

Rover—Play a standup 5 technique. If the option shows to your side, you come down hard to take the quarterback; don't feather him, make him pitch quick. On plays away from you, trail as deep as the ball.

Strong Tackle—Line up on the inside shoulder of the tight end. On the snap, you must explode down the line of scrimmage, with your eyes focusing on the quarterback. You must beat the tight end across the line of scrimmage and not allow him to get his head to your inside pad and block you off your path. If the quarterback decides to pull the ball on the option, you should make contact just as he comes off of his ride to the fullback. If the belly play is called, the quarterback will step down the line and then back toward the offside halfback. When you recognize this play, adjust your angle to the back with the ball.

Nose—Line up in a 2 technique on the strong side guard. On the snap, use the dart technique to the strong side, looking for the fullback.

Weak Tackle—Play a 3 technique.

Sam—Play a standup 1 technique to the tight end side. Hang inside for the fullback as the nose guard is darting to the outside. If the nose guard is doubled by the guard and tackle and the fullback breaks outside, you must scrape out and make the play. Remember, your depth must be such that you can step up inside or outside to take the fullback. When this stunt is called, you must key the fullback all the way.

Willie—Play a standup 1 technique to the split end side.

Secondary—When we play 70 Wide-Go we will play a "special" coverage. Due to the fact that we have all three phases of the triple option covered to the tight end side, we can overshift our secondary in order to get extra support to the split end side.

Strong Safety—Line up closer to the rover end than you normally would in 1 coverage. Read the release of the near back and the flow. If the flow is away from you, rotate back through the deep middle, helping on the quick pass to the split end. If the flow is to you and the near back is releasing toward the defensive end, you should squat to make sure the quarterback does not get away from the rover. If the near back releases in an arc to block on you, get up field quickly to take the pitch, knowing you will have help from the corner.

Strong Corner—(corner to the side of the strong safety) Line up six and a half yards deep on the outside shoulder of the split end. If the flow is away from you, play 1 coverage; you have the deep third to your side. If the flow is to you, bump the receiver to the inside as you watch the play develop. If a run play is coming your way, you must support from the outside.

Free Safety—Line up on the offensive guard to the split end side, twelve yards deep, and key the ball. If the flow is to the split end side, you must be able to cover the deep half of the field to this side. If the flow is to the tight side, rotate back as you would in 1 coverage and look for the tight end running a fly pattern.

Weak Corner—(corner away from the side of the strong safety) Line up two yards deeper and on the outside shoulder of the tight end, as opposed to 1 coverage, when you are two yards outside and five yards deep. On the flow to your side, you must deliver a blow to the end and support as you would on 1 coverage. On a flow away, you have the deep half of the field to your side.

The 70 Wide-Go with special coverage against the Wishbone has proven effective against excellent Southeastern Conference teams and also at the high school level. The outstanding feature of this defense is the fact that you appear to overload to the tight end side, when actually the split end side is the one that is overloaded with defensive personnel.

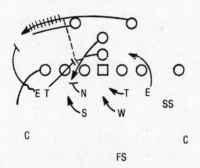

Figure 4-20

THE 40 DEFENSE

The 40 Defense against the Wishbone can be played in certain situations and as a change of pace defense. The 40 Defense is somewhat vulnerable to the cutback and Belly Play unless you have two great defensive linemen playing inside. We use the 40 in passing situations and with only a few seconds to go before half time or the end of the game.

We will at times use what we refer to as a Sam Stack to the tight end side in order to cover up who has the dive and/or the quarterback. The end to the strong side will line up on the inside shoulder of the tight end, with Sam directly behind him. On the snap, the man who has the dive must come flat down the line for the fullback. The player who has the quarterback steps to the outside and feels the tight end's block. This call will never be played straight, because it would involve teaching a 7 technique to the end. One of the players in the stack will go down hard to take the dive, and the other will step outside to take the quarterback. (See Figure 4-21.)

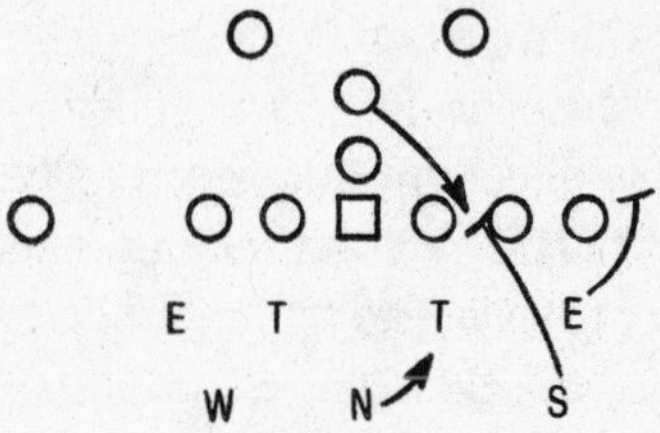

Figure 4-21

We utilize a Weak Slant combined with the Sam Stack to help us against the cutback play. (See Figure 4-22.) The nose guard must be ready to fill the center-guard gap if flow is to the slant and scrape around the slanting tackle if flow is away from the slant.

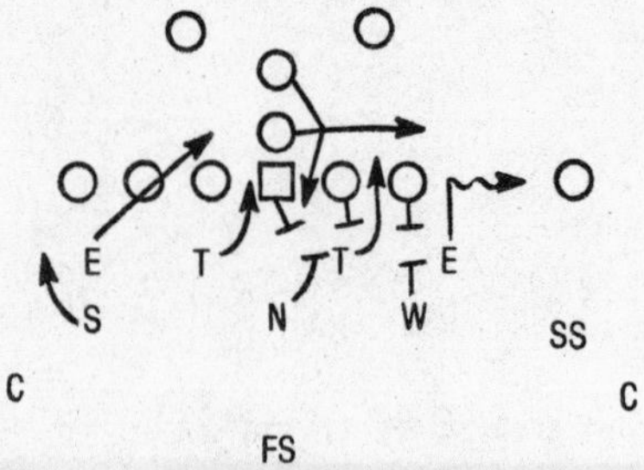

Figure 4-22

When we use a Strong Slant, it is in anticipation of a belly play, sweep, or lead to the tight end side. The Sam Stack will not be used to the tight end side if we call the Strong Slant. The end and Sam play their normal 40 techniques. (See Figure 4-23.) The nose guard, again, must fill or scrape, depending on the flow.

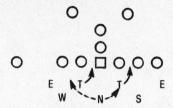

Figure 4-23

The 40 Dog Stunt, which is used to the weak side, is a change-up between the end and Willie linebacker. The end should drive through the hip of the offensive tackle and take the fullback on the flow to him. If the flow is away, he will trail as deep as the ball. The Willie linebacker will be in his 40 alignment and key the fullback-near back triangle. If the flow is to him, he will read and then scrape outside to the quarterback. (See Figure 4-24.) If the flow is away, he will work for the cutback or counter play. This stunt involves only the weak side end and Willie linebacker.

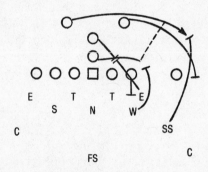

Figure 4-24

The Dog Stunt and a strong slant can be combined to keep pressure on plays to the strong side and also to give a change-up to the split end side. This stunt can also provide a good pass rush in throwing situations.

CHAPTER 5

USING THE MULTIPLE SCHEME TO
DEFEND AGAINST THE WINGED T

The use of a flanker or wing in offensive football goes back to the early 1920's, when Lou Little used what he called a Winged T formation at Columbia University. The University of Iowa under Forest Evashevski enjoyed tremendous success with the Winged T formation from 1956 through 1960, winning three Big Ten titles and two Rose Bowl games within a five year period. In more recent years, the University of Delaware has run this offense with outstanding results.

The Winged T formation borrowed principles from two former offensive schemes: Single Wing blocking patterns and the Split T backfield action. This offense was adopted for two reasons: to reduce the pressure on the center and to have the quick hitting capabilities of the T formation.

The plays that make up the basic Winged T formation are the dive to the halfback, the slant by the fullback, the option of the wing, the sweep, and misdirection plays. The six basic plays that we will be concerned with in this chapter are shown in Figure 5-1 through 5-6.

THE 50 DEFENSE AND THE WINGED T

We must be able to play the 50 against any and all formations with a minimum number of changes for the defensive personnel. Because of the type of plays that are run from this formation, most of the adjustments will be a change in keys rather than technique changes. Each position in the 50 will be played as follows:

Anchor End—Line up in a 9 technique on the end to the wing side. On the snap, jam the end with a shiver and feel the block of the wingback. You should be able to see the wing out of the corner of your eye. If the end blocks down and the wing tries to seal you to the inside, you must take a short jab step with the inside foot as you hit the tight end and then a lateral step with the outside foot as you work across the wingback's face. (See Figure 5-7.) On a drop back pass, you will contain the rush.

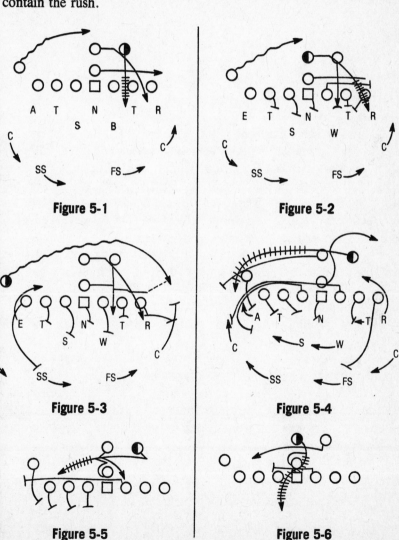

Figure 5-1

Figure 5-2

Figure 5-3

Figure 5-4

Figure 5-5

Figure 5-6

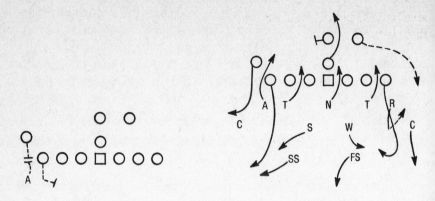

Figure 5-7   **Figure 5-8**

Rover—The rover will not see a tight wing unless there is a double wing formation. If faced with this situation, the rover will play in the manner described for the anchor end. On a drop back pass, the rover will work to the hook area, keying the near back's route as he drops. (See Figure 5-8.) The rover must always be aware of the threat of a reverse when the wing is away from him. The rover will play a 9 technique and key the tight end and near back.

Left Tackle—Play a 5 technique. When facing this formation, you must realize that integral parts of the offense include traps and counter plays. You must prepare yourself to play trap blocks, down blocks, and double team blocks.

Right Tackle—Play the 5 technique as described for the left tackle.

Nose Guard—Play a 0 technique two to three feet off the ball and read the center. Be alert for double team blocks on the trap plays.

Sam—Play a standup 3 technique on the guard to the strong side. Because of misdirection plays, the Sam cannot effectively key a back; he must go to a guard key and react to the different type of blocks shown by the guard.

Willie—The weak side linebacker will read the guard keys as described for Sam. On a drop back pass, Willie must read the tailback as he works to the middle area. If the back runs a flare or flat route, Willie must come off the middle and go to curl. (See Figure 5-9.)

Secondary—The techniques that will be discussed under each position will be for our 1 coverage. Any changes made by the defensive backfield because of an alignment up front will be explained under that particular set.

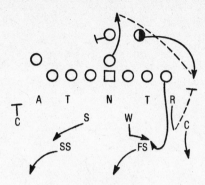

Figure 5-9

Strong Safety—Align in a position over the tackle to the side of the wing where you can cover the outside third. (See Figure 5-10.) When you get motion by the wingback away from you, move to a position over the ball and twelve to fourteen yards deep. You will now take the middle third on drop back passes and still have the outside third if sprint out or action passes show to the side where the wingback first lined up. (See Figure 5-11.)

Free Safety—Your alignment will be to the weak side of the formation, twelve to fourteen yards deep, and in a position to cover either the deep middle or outside third. Against motion, you will have to come to an invert position two yards outside of the tight end and six yards deep. On a flow away, rotate back through the middle. On a run

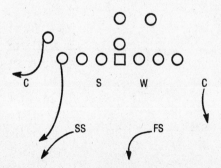

Figure 5-10

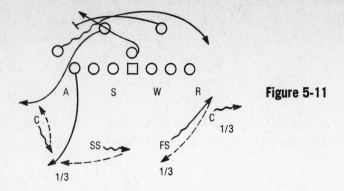

Figure 5-11

action your way, support just outside the end. On a drop back pass, you take the flat.

Strong Corner—Your alignment should be two yards outside the wingback and four yards deep. You should key the wing and end to your side and the ball. If motion occurs away from you, move back to a depth of six yards and key the ball and the end to your side. If the run action shows your way, support to the outside and be ready to take on the block of a guard. You must squeeze everything to the inside as tightly as possible.

Weak Corner—The weak corner will line up three yards outside the end and five yards deep. If motion comes to his side, he must move to the outside when the motion man gets past the end. He will get depth as he moves to the outside and cover the deep third on run or pass.

50 STRONG SLANT-HANG (See Figure 5-12)

This call is one of the best from the 50 Defense because it can help us to put strength against strength and it allows our linebackers freedom of movement that doesn't exist when we play Base 50.

The Strong Slant can be changed from one side to the other when the offense uses motion. The Sam linebacker will change the formation once the wingback begins the motion. For example, in Figure 5-12 the Sam linebacker would call "Strong Left" once the offense took their positions, but when motion starts back across he would yell "Strong Right" and the interior people would have to change their slants to the right.

The Strong Slant-Hang is different from our regular Strong Slant in that the end to the side of the call must not drop off. The end will continue to play his regular 9 technique. The Strong Slant-Hang should be called in definite running situations. If a pass play develops, there will be five players rushing the quarterback and six people defending, which will leave one zone open.

Only the techniques for the nose guard, the linebackers, and the tackles will be discussed, because there will be no change for the ends and secondary when this stunt is called. Most of these changes will be coaching points that will be stressed during the week of practice rather than changes in technique.

Strong Tackle—At the snap, take a short lateral step to the tight end and read the offensive tackle as you go. If the tackle is blocking down, close back to the inside, and look for a trap. If the tackle is turning out on you, run around him and close back because the tackle is slanting outside and it is impossible to slant and work inside. If the offensive blocker turns out, we ask the tackle to run around. If the tackle was playing his regular 5 technique he would work through the blockers head. Stay low as you step to the tight end. If you feel him blocking down on you, work across his face as you locate the ball. If the tackle is reaching to your outside, use your inside shoulder to come through his head and locate the ball.

Weak Tackle—On the movement of the ball, the tackle to the weak side of the formation should take a short step with the inside foot, take a crossover step with the outside foot, and aim for the shoulder of the offensive guard. As he steps, he should pick up the guard's action. If the offensive lineman is firing straight out, the tackle should hit the guard's outside pad and look inside for a trap. When the guard pulls in the direction of the slant, the tackle should get in his hip pocket and go with him. If the guard pulls away from the direction of the slant, the tackle should come back around the offensive tackle as tight to the line of scrimmage as possible.

Nose—The nose guard will feel the block of the center and read the guard to the side of the slant. On the snap, the nose guard will take a short lateral step and club the center with the onside hand. As he breaks the line of scrimmage, the nose guard should pick up the block of the guard. If the guard is pulling in the direction of the slant, the nose guard should go with him. If the guard pulls away from the slant, the nose guard should come back around the center. If the guard is blocking straight out, the nose guard should react to the flow of the ball.

Sam Linebacker—Sam should be ready to fill if the guard blocks down on the nose guard. Sam must also be ready to scrape around the nose guard if the guard blocks straight out and the flow goes to the weak side.

Willie—If the flow is to the weak side of formation and the guard blocks straight out, Willie should scrape just outside of his tackle.

The Strong Slant-Hang is a good defense against the Winged T formation because the offense must adjust the blocking patterns to take care of the interior linemen. A number of teams play the slant as their basic defense against all offensive formations and are well pleased with its effectiveness.

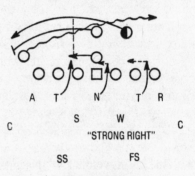

Figure 5-12

50 STACK (See Figure 5-13.)

The 50 Stack that we employ at Mississippi State is a take off on the monster defense that was so popular in the 50's. This defense will help on the plays to the strong side and eliminate some of the plays that require the guards to pull. The Stack can be run in any situation, but we use it as a defense against the run and as a blitzing defense. This defense is moved into from the Base 50. The responsibilities for each position are as follows:

Anchor—Play a tight 9 technique, and don't let the end release inside on the stacked linebacker. On a sprint out pass, you must contain.

Rover—Play your regular 9 technique.

Strong Tackle—Play a 3 technique.

Weak Tackle—Play a 5 technique.

Nose—Play a 2 technique on the weak side guard.

Sam—Play a standup 1 technique.

Willie—Play a standup 1 technique.

Strong Corner—Come to the line of scrimmage one yard outside of the wingback and one yard deep. Key the wing and the flow of the ball. If the flow is away, you must rotate back through the deep third. If motion goes away from you, move back to a depth of four yards.

Strong Safety—Play 1 coverage.

Free Safety—Play 1 coverage.

Weak Corner—Play 1 coverage.

The dive play should be stopped because you have three defensive men on two offensive blockers. The Willie linebacker must keep leverage on the ball as he scrapes down the line to check the dive and the fullback. In Figure 5-13 the defense has the blockers outnumbered at the point of attack. The offense must also decide whether to pull the guard or not. (See Figure 5-2.) If the offense runs this particular play against this defensive set, they must change some blocking assignments or cancel the play.

In Figure 5-13, the Willie linebacker should be able to help on the option. The rover end should take the quarterback, the free safety will take the pitch, and Willie will scrape to the ball. In Figure 5-14, the corner must turn the sweep to the inside. The anchor end must keep Sam free to scrape off the tackle and close the seam between the corner and the defensive end.

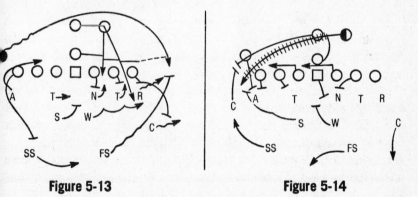

Figure 5-13   **Figure 5-14**

If a trap play is run to the strong side, the defensive tackle must deliver a blow to the offensive guard and step laterally to meet the trapping guard. The nose guard should play back into the center's block, and the two inside linebackers must hang inside anytime the quarterback is spinning behind the center.

If a drop back pass shows, the responsibilities for each player remain the same as in Base 50. The pass rush lanes for the defensive linemen are even better than in the 50, because they are already lined up in the lanes. (See Figure 5-15.)

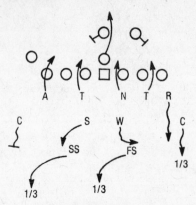

Figure 5-15

50 STACK BLITZ (See Figure 5-16)

When we use the 50 Stack Defense, we want to be able to apply pressure on the offense and force a mistake. In certain throwing situations, we will blitz from the stack, look, and attempt to put the offense in a lead situation. The blitz has also been very effective against counters, options, and traps. The sweep can hurt this blitz if the ball can be brought to the outside quickly, away from all the stunts. The 50 Stack Blitz is shown in Figure 5-16 against a drop back pass. If the defense should anticipate the fullback releasing on a route, use either an end or a linebacker.

The 3 technique tackles and the nose guard stunts through the guard-center gaps, while the linebackers hit the guard-tackle gaps. The weak side tackle uses a slant technique to the outside in order to help widen the area that Willie stunts through. If an end is to be held on the line of scrimmage to check for a back, it is better to hold the rover in order to balance the number of people rushing from each side. In Figure 5-16, the rover will take the tailback and the free safety will cheat head up on the ball, ten yards deep, and take the fullback to either side. The free safety will also help on the tailback if the fullback blocks and the tailback comes to the strong side.

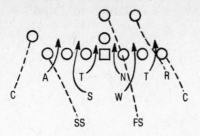

Figure 5-16

50 SLIDE (See Figure 5-17)

This defense has been used in high school football with a certain amount of success against offensive formations that feature a wing. The 50 Slide should be used against a team that uses a split end constantly and runs the sweep and counter plays to the strong side as their bread-and-butter plays. The 50 Slide cannot be run against two tight ends, because the defense would be vulnerable to the rover end side. If 50 Slide has been called in the huddle and the offense has lined up in a two tight end situation, the Sam linebacker must check the defense. He can check to Base 50 or 50 Stack. The 50 Slide is shown in Figure 5-17 against a Winged T formation with a split end.

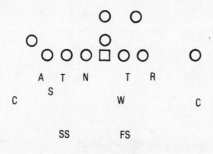

Figure 5-17

This defense should be extremely strong against the run game to the strong side. It is very similar to the 70 Defense. The big difference between the 50 Slide and the 70 Defense is the position of the strong linebacker. In a 50 Slide, Sam will play in a standup 7 technique as he does in the 53 Stack Defense. On a flow to him, he will scrape around the defensive end to close the seam between the corner and the defen sive end. If the wingback blocks on Sam, the end will be free to work outside in this area. (See Figure 5-18.)

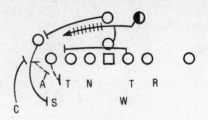

Figure 5-18

The nose guard must do a good job of playing the quick traps from his 2 technique since he will not have the Sam linebacker to help him as he did in the 70 Defense. This position is probably more vulnerable than any other because there is no overlap from the linebackers.

The strong side tackle will play a 5 technique as he does in the 50 Defense. He will rush to the inside on a drop back pass in order to help on the draw.

The weak side tackle, Willie, and rover will play the same techniques as they did in the 70 Defense. The rover end will have no pass coverage responsibility. He is to rush from the outside and contain the quarterback.

The 50 Slide should be used in running situations or when the offensive tendencies indicate that only six zones of the field need to be covered. This defense can provide strength to the formation side, and it lends itself well to the different stunts and blitzes that will be discussed next.

50 SLIDE FIRE (See Figure 5-19)

This stunt is a great change-up for the defense to the strength of the offense and is an exceptional call against the sweep, counter, trap, and sprint pass to the wingback. The secondary will play man coverage, with the Willie linebacker taking the fullback.

The anchor end should loosen slightly from his regular 9 technique and take a short lateral step for the wingback when the ball is snapped. The anchor must pull the quarterback up on the play as shown in Figure 5-19.

The strong side tackle will execute a slant technique to the outside. He must not allow himself to be blocked in by the offensive tackle. He should be the person who applies the quick pressure on the quarterback when the sprint pass is run.

Sam should cheat to the inside eye of the end and on the snap of the ball take a step with the inside foot and hit the guard-tackle gap to his side. If a counterplay has been called against this stunt, the Sam linebacker should cause the offense a few problems. Often, this linebacker will hit the quarterback and shake the ball loose.

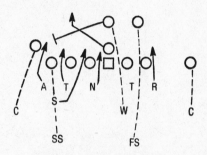

Figure 5-19

50 SLIDE RUSH (See Figure 5-20)

Whereas the 50 Slide Fire was primarily a running play call to help on certain plays to the strong side of the formation, the 50 Slide Rush is a call designed to put a maximum rush on the quarterback in throwing situations. We will use this stunt primarily against a straightback passer or one who doesn't run very well, because a defense can be hurt if the quarterback gets outside the rush. The 50 Slide Fire and the 50 Slide Rush are the same for the front people to the strong side of formation. The Willie linebacker, weak side tackle, and rover techniques are different, and the secondary plays man for man coverage. The 50 Slide Rush is shown in Figure 5-20.

The Willie linebacker should shoot the center-guard gap on the snap of the ball. He should be anticipating the center's block and take the block on with the shoulder nearest the center.

On the snap of the ball, the weak side tackle should take a lateral step with the outside foot and get upfield. The guard should never be able to reach block him if a running play occurs to his side.

When the ball is snapped, the rover end should read run or pass. If he reads straight back pass, he should come upfield, making sure the quarterback does not break containment.

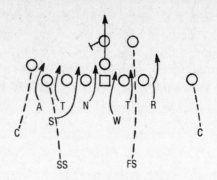

Figure 5-20

50 SLIDE-SLANT (See Figure 5-21)

This call has been very good against inside plays and also on running plays to the split end side of the formation. We have sealed off all gaps to the inside and have overlap help from the linebacker to the weak side.

Normally, we do not favor the linebackers keying the backs in the Wing T as we do in certain other formations because of misdirection plays. However, we will key the Willie linebacker on the flow of the ball when this defensive call is made in order to determine the direction he must scrape.

Anchor End—Line up in a tight 9 technique. On the snap, take a short step laterally with the inside foot and drive through the end-tackle gap to your side.

Rover—Your alignment will be a standup 5 technique to the split end side. You must come down hard at a point behind where the offensive tackle lined up. Your movement begins when the ball is snapped.

S.T.—Line up in a 5 technique and execute a slant to the inside of the offensive tackle.

W.T.—Line up in a tight 3 technique and slant to the inside of the offensive guard on the snap.

Nose—Line up in a 2 technique on the guard to the strong side and dart to the guard-center gap.

Sam—Align on the outside eye of the end to the side of the wing

On the snap, you must step to the outside and anticipate the wing's block. If the wingback blocks on the end, you must be ready for a pulling guard.

Willie—You must be set in a standup 1 technique to the split end side. The key to your position is the quarterback and the flow of the ball. If the quarterback is spinning or steps to the weak side, you must scrape to the outside. If the quarterback and both backs go the strong side, you should work behind the line of scrimmage and be ready for the cutback.

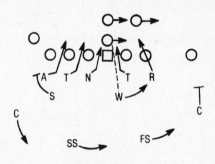

Figure 5-21

THE 53 STACK AGAINST THE WINGED T (See Figure 5-22)

The 53 Stack can be run very effectively against the Winged T whether the offense has a split end or not. This defense can eliminate some of the plays that require the guards to pull because of the stack over the center and the threat of stunts. The secondary will play man coverage, and to a certain extent this is the weakness of the defense. Play action passes with crossing receivers can hurt your team unless the secondary works very hard to play the receivers first and then react to the ball.

The fullback slant will be the responsibility of Willie, the nose guard, the defensive end, and the tackle. This defense can force the offense to keep the guard in to block the Willie linebacker, expecially if the dart stunt is used occasionally.

In Figure 5-23 the defensive end will take on the block of the offensive end and begin to work back through the pressure. Once the offensive end releases this block, the 9 technique should recognize the option and begin to open up to the outside to help on the quarterback.

The strong safety, if the flow is to his side, and the offensive end blocking should scrape to the outside to take the quarterback. When the corner sees the end block, he should immediately come up to a position that will allow him to take the pitch. If the corner reads correctly, he will beat the block of the end.

When a counter or sweep is run to the strong side and the offensive end blocks down, the defensive end will deliver a blow and then step to the outside and read the play. If the wing does not block on him and he sees a guard pulling to block him out, he must close back to the inside. The Sam linebacker must read the flow and the block of the tight end. If the tight end is blocking down to the inside and the flow is to him, he must scrape to the inside shoulder of the wing. If the flow is away and the tight end blocks out on the defensive end, Sam must hang inside.

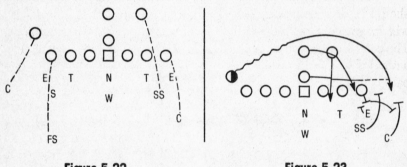

Figure 5-22   Figure 5-23

THE 80 DEFENSE AND THE WINGED T (See Figure 5-24)

The 80 Defense has been good to us because of the difficult blocking angles it presents to the offense. This defense will also limit, to a certain extent, plays that involve pulling the guards. If the offense does pull the guards, certain stunts involving the four defensive players to the inside should be very effective.

When this defense is faced with stopping the dive-option series away from the wing, the techniques and responsibilities are as follows. The secondary will be playing man for man coverage.

When the dive play is run, the inside people must make the play. The tackles can never be blocked to the inside by the guard, and the linebacker must keep leverage on the football at all times. Sometimes, a linebacker will make the mistake of getting up too tight to his tackle and will get tied up before he can scrape to the ball. His depth should be around four yards from the ball. The linebacker away from the flow of the ball should make the play if the back cuts back inside the defensive tackle. The strong safety will not begin his scrape to this outside until after he is sure the dive back does not have the ball. If the back has the ball, the strong safety will give help inside. If the ball is pulled, the strong safety will scrape immediately for the pitch.

If the off-tackle play to the fullback has been called, the defensive end must do a good job of squeezing the play. The strong safety will scrape to the outside for the pitch, which will leave a hole inside the end unless he jams the tight end and closes down tight to the inside. As he works inside, the end must be prepared to meet the pulling guard with his shoulders square and not be turned out.

When the offense runs the option to the side of motion, the play should be defended with the end on the quarterback. The free safety will move across with the motion and key the tight end for the pass. The defensive end must not allow the tight end to widen him and create a running lane to his inside. He must take the quarterback and force the ball to be pitched.

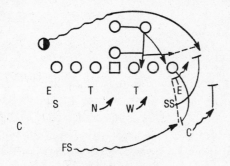

Figure 5-24

80 OUT (See Figure 5-25)

This call is good against any offense that tried to reach block the defensive tackles with the offensive guards. Once the offensive team is forced to block down with the tackles, the inside linebackers are free to scrape to the ball. This call only concerns the four inside people. The tackles take a short jab step with the outside foot toward the offensive blocker to their outside, anticipating a down block. As the tackles step, they should read the guards release off the line of scrimmage. If the guard is trying to get his head outside of the 3 technique, the tackle should work upfield for penetration into the backfield. If the guard is blocking down inside, the tackle should close back to the inside as quickly as possible and get tight to the line of scrimmage as he pursues the ball.

Both linebackers must realize the vulnerable spot of the defense is inside, and if this area is threatened they must be prepared to hang inside. If the ball goes outside quickly, they can scrape outside in normal fashion.

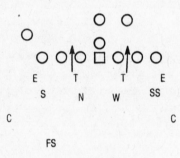

Figure 5-25

80 SLIDE (See Figure 5-26)

This call is used in short yardage-goal line situations or when a maximum rush is wanted on the quarterback. The secondary will be in man coverage, with the Willie linebacker covering the fullback. The Willie linebacker can be added to the rush if you are willing to gamble that the offense will not sneak the fullback out on a pass route. The 80 Slide is shown in Figure 5-26 against the Winged T.

The 80 Slide is an excellent call inside the ten yard line when the 80 Defense has been used previously. There are only two positions that will be required to assume different alignments. The Sam linebacker will drop to a three point stance in the gap between the end and tackle to the formation side. The nose guard will move head up on the center. The assignments for all positions are as follows:

Anchor—Line up in a 9 technique and fire over the outside shoulder of the end on the snap.

Rover—Same alignment and responsibility as the anchor end.

Strong Tackle—Align in a 3 technique and fire the guard-tackle gap.

Weak Tackle—Same as the strong tackle.

Nose—Line up in the 80 Defense, but on a command of "move" by Sam drop to a 0 technique and execute a dart to the side of the Sam linebacker.

Sam—Show your normal 80 alignment at first, but when the quarterback begins his cadence drop to a three point stance and fire the end-tackle gap on the snap of the ball.

Willie—Regular 80 alignment. You have the fullback man to man on all passes unless you figure in the rush.

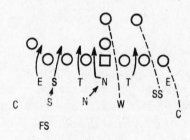

Figure 5-26

CHAPTER 6

THE SLOT I AND
MULTIPLE DEFENSIVE SETS

We must analyze and understand the philosophy of each offensive formation before we can properly defend against it. We must know the strong and weak points and plan accordingly. The Slot I utilizes one good ball carrier to the fullest extent. Several college teams, such as Ohio State with Archie Griffin and U.S.C. with Ricky Bell, have used the Slot I with tremendous success in recent years.

The defense, therefore, must be prepared to defend against the opponent's best running back at all points along the line of scrimmage. (See Figure 6-1.) Remembering this one fact can sometimes prevent a defense from overloading to the side at which they anticipate the attack.

Our philosophy against the Slot I is to make sure we can stop the running game, force the offense to throw, and then put a heavy rush on the quarterback. If we can consistently stop the running game, the offense must attempt to move the ball by way of the passing game. Once this occurs, we can exert great pressure on the passer through the use of rushes that may consist of as many as eight players or a few as three.

The 50 Defense is played against this formation with the defensive front playing their normal techniques. The linebackers must be given a guard-near back key. This means that the primary key is the type of block the guard shows and the secondary key is the near back to determine the flow of the ball. We try to play the 50 Defense, without stunting, forty to fifty percent of the time.

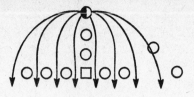

Figure 6-1

50 STRONG SLANT-STAY

This is a very good call against Slot I team that runs the isolation play several times in a game. Once the opponent's offensive tendencies have been established, this call should be made when an inside run play is indicated. Generally, this should occur on first and ten, second and five, or in a situation where the offense expects to gain three yards or more and remain on schedule for a first down.

The defensive tackle must do a good job of delivering a blow to the offensive lineman and limiting the running lane between himself and the near linebacker. The Sam linebacker must take the fullback on with the inside shoulder pad and make the tailback break inside toward the Willie linebacker as shown in Figure 6-2. As the nose guard slants to the strong side, he must look for the offensive guard. The nose guard should drop his outside shoulder pad and deliver a blow so as to create a stalemate and limit the running lane. He must never be driven back off the line of scrimmage. With the defensive tackle working from the outside, the nose guard from the inside, and the linebacker at the point of attack, the isolation play should gain very few yards.

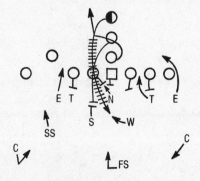

Figure 6-2

The Strong Slant-Stay is also a good call against a team that features the off-tackle play to the tailback away from the slot side. This play is very effective against the 50 Defense unless your linebackers play well.

As stated earlier in this chapter, the linebackers are given a guard-near back key. Each linebacker must also know what the defensive linemen to either side of his position will be doing on the snap of the ball. When a Strong Slant-Stay is called, the Willie linebacker knows that the defensive tackle to his side must come down hard to the inside. Knowing that he should receive help against an inside play permits the Willie linebacker to scrape or fill depending on the flow of the ball. If the flow is to the strength of the formation, Willie must be prepared to fill the area as shown in Figure 6-3. If the flow is away from the formation side, Willie should scrape around the slant tackle

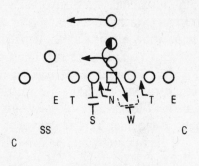

Figure 6-3

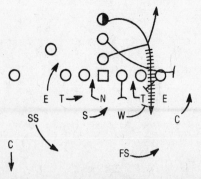

Figure 6-4

and help in the off-tackle hole or outside as shown in Figure 6-4. The secondary will play a zone call in conjunction with the Strong Slant-Stay.

50 DOUBLE STACK

The 50 Double Stack is similar in many ways to the 50 Stack. The differences between the two calls are the alignments of the nose guard, the two linebackers, and the anchor end. Whereas the nose guard played a 2 technique in the 50 Stack, he now must play a 1 technique to the tight end side. The anchor end must play a standup 5 technique to the split end side of the formation. Both linebackers must be stacked directly behind the nose guard and strong side tackle at a depth of three yards. The linebackers' key is the flow of the football. If the offense gives what we refer to as a split flow, the linebackers must hang inside and locate the ball. A split flow occurs when one back goes in one direction and the other back goes in the opposite direction.

The 50 Double Stack is a good call at any time and in almost any situation because the defense helps to conceal the linebackers and you can still drop the rover end on the pass coverage. The pass coverage and rush lanes are basically the same as in Base 50 because the tackle to the rover side has to contain the rush. This is somewhat of a special defense because it violates the basic rule concerning the rover and anchor ends. Most of the time the rover goes to the open side of the formation and the anchor end goes to the tight end side, but in the Double Stack the rover should go to the tight end side and the anchor should go to the split end side. We want the rover end to drop on the pass coverage and the anchor end to rush. In order for our ends to be able to accomplish this objective when we run the Double Stack, we must violate the basic rule.

The Double Stack is a defense that is easily concealed prior to the snap. On a command by the signal caller, the four inside people slide to their respective positions. The linebacker who calls the defenses should be aware that this defense should be checked to Base 50 if the offense comes out in a two tight end formation, because the defensive end would be outflanked by an offensive blocker otherwise. (See Figure 6-5.)

The key to the defense is how well the nose guard and tackle keep the linebackers free to go to the ball. The nose guard and tackle must force the offense to double team them if the ball is coming to their side. This will limit the number of plays that the offense will have at their disposal. If the opposing team does not double team these linemen, they should present quite a problem to the offensive blockers.

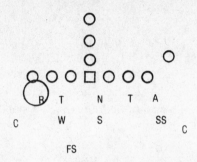

Figure 6-5

The Double Stack is very effective against a slot I team that runs the basic plays from this formation. The isolation, sprint draw, counter, and off tackle plays by the tailback are the guts of the running game from the slot I formation. The passing game from this formation must consist of the sprint out and play action passes.

In Figures 6-6 the off-tackle play by the tailback is shown. The Willie linebacker should key the fullback when he is stacked behind a defensive lineman. It is almost impossible to use the guard key because the offensive linemen will not give a true key when the defense is aligned in the Double Stack. When the play in Figure 6-6 is run, the Willie linebacker must scrape off tackle and close the seam between the tackle end. The Sam linebacker should also key the fullback and move to close down the cutback area between the 3 technique and the nose guard. The defensive end must deliver a blow to the tight end and attempt to keep him from blocking down on the linebacker. After he jams the tight end, the 9 technique must take the fullback's block on with the inside shoulder pad and limit the running lane for the tailback. The defensive end must always strive to keep the outside shoulder and leg free in order to make the tackle if the tailback bounces outside.

Since the linebackers are the key to the Double Stack defense, they must be aware of the fact that the offense will try to pull them out of position by the use of misdirection plays. These players must stay at home whenever the quarterback is spinning behind the center and the backs are giving a split flow. The depth of the linebackers is very important because they need a fraction of a second to read the play. If they get closer than three yards to the line of scrimmage, it is possible that they will get tied up by fakes or blockers before they can locate the point of attack.

In Figure 6-7, the sprint pass is shown against the Double Stack. The strong safety should work to the outside to take away the out cut by either of the wide recievers, with the Sam linebacker going to the curl. The Willie linebacker must work the middle area, looking for crossing routes, and the Rover end should work the backside curl.

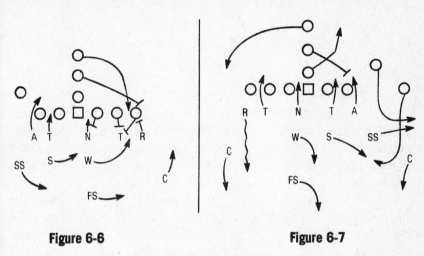

Figure 6-6   Figure 6-7

50 DOUBLE STACK RUSH

The Double-Stack is a reading, pursuing type of defense with only one position, the nose guard, attempting to achieve any penetration. In keeping with our philosophy of concealing the intent of the defense until the snap of the ball, we have an all-out stunting, penetrating rush from the Double Stack. This rush has proven to be effective in short yardage situations and against counter plays and the sprint out pass to the strong side. The responsibilities for each position in the Double Stack Rush are as follows:

Anchor—Play a standup 5 technique to the open side of the formation. On the snap, come through the offensive tackles hip and key the quarterback as you rush. If the quarterback comes down the line, tackle him high and attempt to strip him of the ball. If the quarterback shows sprint out action, try to get some depth and come upfield in order to close down the seam between you and the strong safety. (See Figure 6-8.)

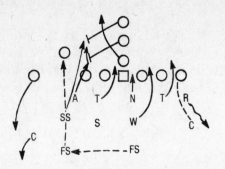

Figure 6-8

Rover—Align yourself to the tight end side of the formation and pick up any back who runs a pass route to your side. If the tailback motions to your side, the cornerback must take him man for man and you should back up two or three yards and take the tight end man for man. (See Figure 6-9.)

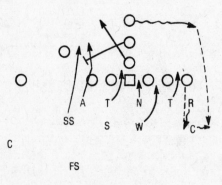

Figure 6-9

Strong Tackle—Line up in a 3 technique and slant inside to the guard-center gap when the ball is snapped.

Weak Tackle—Execute a slant to the outside from your normal 50 alignment. If an option occurs, you must take quarterback. (See Figure 6-10.) If a drop back pass shows, you must contain the quarterback to your side.

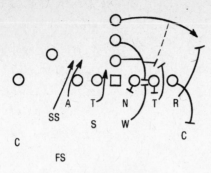

Figure 6-10

Nose—Play a 1 technique and attempt to split the block if a double team occurs.

Sam—Play a standup 1 technique to the strong side of the formation and key the tailback. If the tailback runs a pass route to your side you must take him man for man. If the tailback goes in motion to the strong side, you move out with him. If the tailback goes in motion to the weak side, you stay in the stack position because the weak corner must pick him up. (See Figure 6-9.)

Willie—You must stack behind the nose guard and rush the guard-tackle gap to your side.

Strong Safety—Line up in the same position as you would when playing 1 coverage. Prior to the snap, cheat to a point three yards outside of the anchor end and come across hard when the play begins. If a sprint out pass occurs, you must pull the quarterback up quickly.

Cornerbacks—Play the widest receiver to your side man to man.

Free Safety—You must take the second receiver to the strong side man to man.

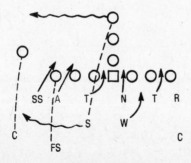

Figure 6-11

The Double Stack Rush can be run against a two tight end formation with only minor adjustments. The anchor end should line up in a 7 technique but rush at the same angle on the snap. The strong safety must line up outside of the tight end one yard and also rush at the angle that is necessary to pull up the quarterback on the sprint pass. The remainder of the defensive personnel will have the same alignments and responsibilities. (See Figure 6-11.)

53 STACK

The 53 Stack will be used against the Slot I formation with two types of secondary play. The call for the front seven people will determine whether the defensive backfield will play zone or man coverage.

This defense should be good against the isolation plays, sweeps, and the sprint out pass to the formation side. The straight drop back pass can hurt the defense since you are committing five or more people to rush the quarterback and will leave one or more zones open.

The tackles in the 53 Stack should play a 4 technique underneath the offensive tackles in order to help on all inside plays. If the defensive tackles cannot be blocked out by the offensive tackles, the offense will have a problem when they are running the isolation and other inside plays. The Willie linebacker must take on the fullback as he does in 50 Defense once he reads the isolation play. This play is shown in Figure 6-12 against the 53 Stack with man for man coverage. In Figure 6-13, the sweep is shown against the 53 Stack using zone coverage.

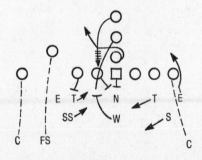

Figure 6-12

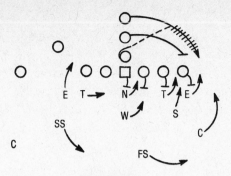

Figure 6-13

The techniques and assignments for the front people will remain the same whether man or zone coverage is called, with one exception, the play of the Sam linebacker. If zone coverage is called, Sam will line up on the inside shoulder of the tight end and key the near back. If the flow is to him, Sam will keep inside-out leverage on the ball, never scraping outside quickly. (See Figure 6-14.) If man coverage has been called, Sam must align himself on the inside eye of the tight end and scrape to the outside on a flow his way. (See Figure 6-15.) The reason for this, of course, is that in zone coverage the cornerback will be the contain portion of the defense if run action shows to the tight end side. In man coverage with the end releasing, the cornerback will have to cover the end and cannot help on the run.

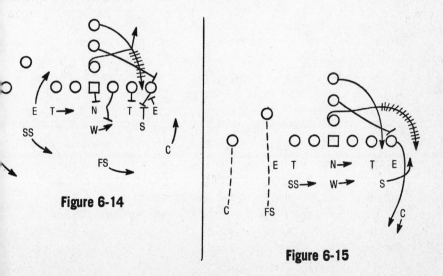

Figure 6-14

Figure 6-15

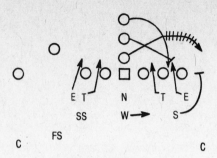

Figure 6-16

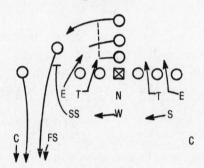

Figure 6-17

53 STACK PINCH (See Figures 6-16 and 6-17)

The Pinch stunt from this defense is an excellent call against the Slot I formation in short yardage situations and situations in which the offensive tendency is to run inside. This stunt also ties in well with the 50 Pinch because the assignments for the personnel are basically the same. The responsibilities for the different positions are as follows:

Anchor—Play a 9 technique. On the snap, come underneath the tight end. Locate the ball as you move.

Rover—Play a 9 technique. On the snap, drive hard for the outside hip of the offensive tackle. Locate the ball as you move.

Strong Tackle—Line up in a 4 technique and drive down hard for the shoulder of the offensive guard next to you.

Nose Guard—Play a 0 technique.

Weak Tackle—Same as the strong tackle.

Sam Linebacker—Play a standup 7 technique and key the ball. If the ball comes to you, scrape outside. If the ball goes away from you, work behind the line of scrimmage.

Willie Linebacker—Play a standup 0 behind the nose guard and key to the ball.

Strong Safety—Play a standup 7 technique. If the flow is to you, scrape to the outside. If the flow is away from you, work behind the line of scrimmage.

Cornerbacks—Play man coverage on the widest receiver to your side.

Free Safety—Play man to man on the second receiver to the strong side of the formation.

The 53 Stack Pinch can be used as an alternate goal line defense when the offense gets inside the ten yard line. This defensive call has provided some big plays for us against some fine offensive teams.

53 STACK SLANT (See Figure 6-18)

The slant from this alignment has been effective against the Slot I sprint series because of the ability of the defense to put quick force on the quarterback and still cover the basic routes.

The interior linemen will slant to the side of the slot back. The end will read the quarterback as he executes a pinch technique, and if sprint out occurs he will get depth and help pull the quarterback up. On the snap of the ball, the strong tackle will slant to the outside and contain. The secondary will play zone coverage, with Sam and Willie taking the curl areas.

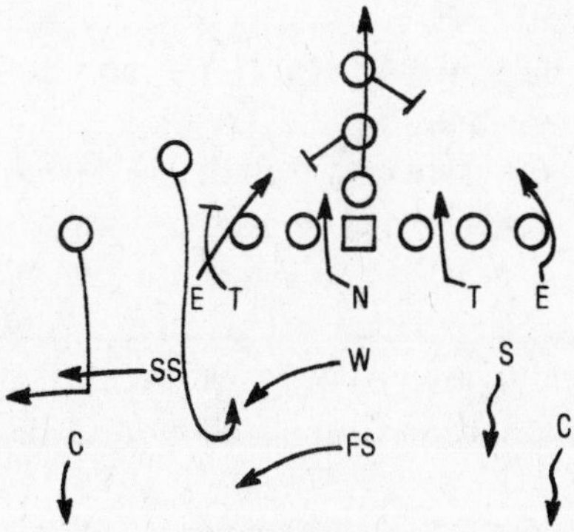

Figure 6-18

This defensive call is very strong against the run in the middle of the formation and to the strong side. The slant is somewhat vulnerable to an option or sweep back to the tight end side because the defense loses some of the pursuit that the slanting linemen would provide.

The 53 Stack Slant is a very good call against a team that uses the inside veer to the formation side a great deal. The end and nose guard must take the dive, with the tackle slanting to the quarterback. A great deal of the time the quarterback will read give because of the slant tackle. The Willie linebacker should overlap the dive also. (See Figure 6-19.)

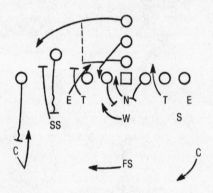

Figure 6-19

40 SLANT (See Figure 6-20)

The 40 Slant is used primarily in a passing situation. Certain types of motion and pass patterns will also force us to use the 40 Defense, although we may not slant each and every time. We believe that the 40 Slant gives us a better outside rush than the 50 defense against the Slot I because neither end is involved in pass coverage.

The 40 Slant can be called to either the strength or weakness of the formation, but when we use it against the Slot I we go to the strength unless we get motion from the tailback. Everyone on defense will play the 40 technique with the exception of the tackles. On the snap of the ball, the tackles will slant to the strength of the formation, reading the blocking pattern as they move. If the flow is to the slant side, the tackles continue in that direction. If the flow is away from the slant, the tackles will run around the block and pursue the ball. The secondary will play zone coverage when the 40 Slant is used. The linebackers in the 40 Slant must know the areas that should be filled when the flow is to them or away from them. If the flow is away from the strength of the formation, the nose guard should scrape around the tackle and fill to the tight end side of the formation. If the flow is to the strength of the formation, the nose guard should be able to fill the guard-center gap. (See Figure 6-21.)

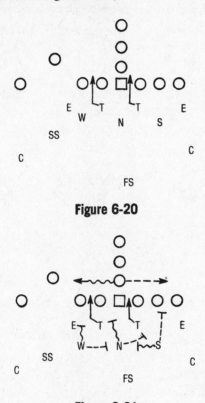

Figure 6-20

Figure 6-21

70 WIDE-SLANT (See Figure 6-22)

The 70 Wide-Slant is used to help on the inside running game while still getting maximum pass coverage on the sprint out series. This call is also excellent against the sprint draw and counter plays to the tailback because of the penetration of the three interior linemen.

Because of the rover end's ability to play pass coverage, the anchor end will go to the split end side and rover will go the tight end side. Once rover reads a pass, he will drop to the weak curl. The secondary will play 1 coverage. The techniques for each position are as follows:

Anchor End—Play a standup 5 technique to the formation side.

Rover—Play a 9 technique to the tight end side. On a pass action, you must take the curl area. If a back is swinging out of the backfield, you must stay in the curl area since the cornerback will take the back once he gets fifteen yards deep.

Strong Tackle—Line up in a 3 technique and use a slant-out technique on the snap of the ball. Anticipate the offensive tackle blocking down on you.

Weak Tackle—Prior to the snap, show a 7 technique alignment. On the snap, drive hard for the outside hip of the opposing tackle, reading the flow as you go. If the run flow is to you, be ready to take on the turnout block from the tackle. If a pass action shows, you will rush on the outside to contain the quarterback.

Nose Guard—Play a 2 technique alignment. On the snap, you must drive the guard-center gap to your side, reading the flow as you penetrate. If the flow is to you, avoid the block of the center and get upfield. If the flow is away from you, flatten down the line of scrimmage as you pursue. (See Figure 6-23.)

Sam—Play a standup 1 technique to the end side. Your key should be the fullback and the flow of the ball. If a sprint pass occurs, you must cover the curl to the strong side.

Willie—Play a standup 1 technique to the split end side and cover the middle on a sprint pass. Be alert for crossing routes by the slot back and the tight end.

Defensive Backfield—Play 1 coverage.

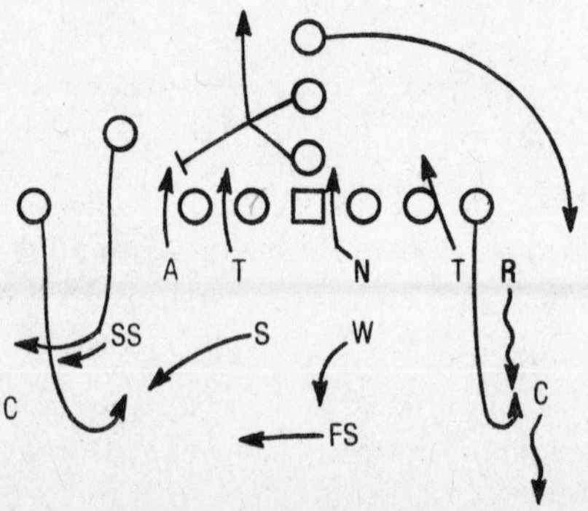

Figure 6-22

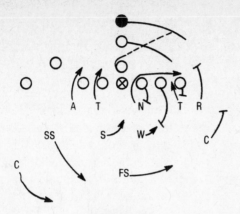

Figure 6-23

80 GO (See Figure 6-24)

This call is made to get a maximum rush from the 80 Defense and to apply pressure to the off-tackle area. The secondary will play man to man coverage, and the two inside linebackers will key the backs. If a back releases on a pass route to the strong side, the Willie linebacker will go with him. The nose guard goes with him if he releases to the weak side. The Sam linebacker will fire the gap between the tight end and offensive tackle if the flow is to his side. The rover end will widen slightly and allow the strong safety to fire between him and the offensive tackle if the flow is to his side.

This call puts tremendous pressure on the off-tackle area and can cause a great deal of confusion in the offensive backfield. The 80 Go is

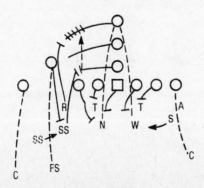

Figure 6-24

an excellent call against the counter option, lead option, or sprint pass when the quarterback is a good runner.

80 X (See Figure 6-25)

The 80 X is a reverse of the 80 Go. Both calls are the same for everyone but the ends, Sam linebacker, and strong safety. The blocking scheme of the offensive team should dictate which one to use. For example, if the slot man uses a crack back block on the strong safety when running the lead option, the 80 Go should be run. (See Figure 6-24.) If the offense uses the counter option with the fullback sealing on the inside linebacker and the tackle reaching for the strong safety, the 80 X should be called.

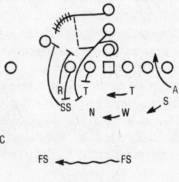

Figure 6-25

The anchor end must come across the face of the tight end on the snap of the ball. The Sam linebacker can either go on the snap or key the flow. If the flow is to him, he must execute the slant. If the flow is away from him, he can work back to the inside as he checks for reverses.

The rover end will drive hard for a point just behind the tackle to his side, looking for quarterback. If the flow is away, he will trail. If a sprint pass occurs, he will get depth, knowing that the strong safety will help to the outside.

The strong safety will play a key stunt, which means that if the flow is to him he will come upfield, keying the quarterback. If the play is the counter option, as shown in Figure 6-25, he will take the pitch man. If the flow is away from him, he works back to the deep middle. (See Figure 6-26.)

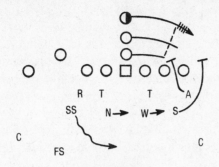

Figure 6-26

The 80 X and 80 Go calls should be used when the offense exhibits a tendency to run outside or off tackle. These calls are not designed to help on the isolation play, although the people stunting to the inside will sometimes recognize a play and come off their primary assignment to make the tackle for no gain. The eight people up front must realize that the secondary is playing man coverage and that when the receiver drives deep they cannot support on the run until the threat of a pass has been abolished. If the triple option is run by the offense, the player who stunts to the inside has the quarterback and the player who goes outside has the pitch. The four inside people must take the dive and cutback.

GOAL LINE DEFENSES VS. THE SLOT I

Our philosophy on defense is that nothing counts except the number of points the opposition puts on the scoreboard. We can't be beaten if our opponents don't score, regardless of the yards gained or passes completed. We want to completely shut down the running game inside the ten yard line and force the opposing team to throw the ball. Once we accomplish this objective, we must apply pressure to the passes and cover the favorite routes of the offense in the four-down zone.

In order to accomplish these objectives, we must instill in our defensive unit the ability to play with a certain amount of controlled fanaticism. We, as a coaching staff, must teach the defensive unit a number of fronts and how to conceal these looks and stunts until the last second.

The big decision to be made by our defensive team is when and where to go into our goal line defense or 60 Defense. This decision should be made based on the down, the distance, the type of goal line offense you face, and the attack pattern of the opponent. Generally, we want to go into our 60 Defense around the five yard line if the offense has two or more downs to score.

When we go into the 60 Defense we want to substitute two big linemen for the nose guard and free safety. We want size at the two inside linemen positions and are not concerned to a great extent with quickness.

60 DEFENSE (See Figure 6-27)

Ends—Play a tough 9 technique. Take the quarterback on the option. You have no pass responsibility.

Tackles—Play a head up position on the offensive tackle. On the snap, you must drive low and hard through the offensive tackle's crotch at an inside angle and try to establish a new line of scrimmage one yard deep in the backfield.

Guards—Play a 1 technique, with your alignment on the shoulder of the center. At the snap, drive hard through the knee of the center and up through the center-guard gap. You must never be driven back. You must achieve penetration.

Linebackers—Align on the outside shoulder of the offensive guard to your side and at a depth that should allow you to scrape behind your lineman. Your key is the flow of the ball and near back. If a pass

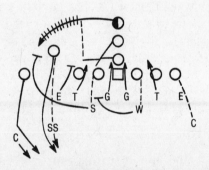

Figure 6-27

action shows, you must take the back out to your side. If an option shows to your side, you have the pitch and the backside linebacker takes the dive.

Cornerbacks—Play man coverage and take the widest receiver to your side.

Strong Safety—Play man to man on the second receiver to the strength of the formation.

60 BLITZ (See Figures 6-28 and 6-29)

In order to keep the offense off balance and apply pressure to the quarterback in a throwing situation, we use the 60 Blitz. This is a good call from the four to five yard line on a third down when you anticipate a pass or an option. The techniques for the secondary and defensive guards remain the same as in the 60 Defense, but the techniques for the linebackers, tackles, and ends change. The techniques for the guards, cornerbacks, and strong safety were discussed earlier in this chapter. The techniques for the linebackers, tackles, and ends are as follows:

Ends—Align in a 9 technique and read the near back. On the

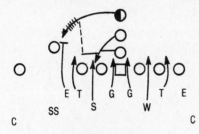

Figure 6-28

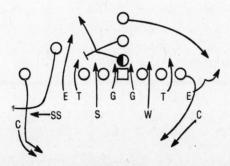

Figure 6-29

snap, take a lateral step to the outside in order to make sure you are not reached by the tight end or tight slot. If an option shows your way, you take the pitch. If a pass action shows, you must take the back out to your side.

Tackles—Align in your regular 60 alignment and slant to the outside on the snap of the ball. You must contain the quarterback on a rollout pass. The only time you should get help on containment is when a back blocks the end on a sprint pass (See Figure 6-29). Against an option play, you must take the quarterback.

Linebackers—Align on the outside shoulder of the offensive guards and fire the guard-tackle gap on the snap of the ball. You take the dive if an option develops.

60 STACK RUSH (See Figure 6-30)

The 60 Stack Rush has been very good to us against a Slot I team that attempts to run the isolation inside, the sweep to the slot side, or the tailback off tackle to the tight end side. The key to this alignment and stunt is to show the 60 Defense and then move to the 60 Stack just prior to the snap. Most of the time the Sam linebacker should come free and cause a great deal of confusion.

Strong Side End—Align in your 60 alignment and key the backs. If a back flares to your side, you must take him because the linebacker is stunting. If both backs block on you, fight through the blockers and pull the quarterback up. You have the pitch on all options your way.

Strong Side Tackle—Align in the 60 Defense and slant to the outside. Take the quarterback on options your way. Pull the quarterback up against a rollout pass with only one back blocking.

Strong Side Guard—Slide from a 1 technique to a head up position on the offensive guard when the linebacker says "Move." On the snap, slant to the guard-tackle gap, trying to stay low and achieve penetration.

Weak Side Guard—Align in a 1 technique. On command, move to a head up position on the center. On the snap, execute a dart to the weak side guard-center gap.

Weak Side Tackle—Align in your regular 60 alignment but execute a slant to the inside on the snap. Stay low and drive hard for the guard-tackle gap.

Weak Side End—Play 60 Defense.

Sam Linebacker—Show 60 Defense. After the quarterback has

begun his cadence, move the defense to the 60 Stack. You should not
have to move since your alignment should help to disguise the stunt.
On the snap, fire the guard-center gap to the strong side.

Willie Linebacker—Position yourself in the gap between the
offensive tight end and tackle. *Read the tight end.* If the tight end
blocks down on the tackle, be ready to step around the defensive end to
take the next threat. If the tight end blocks out, step up to take on the
fullback in the lead play. (See Figure 6-31.) On a pass, you take the
back that comes out to your side.

Secondary—Play man coverage on the three remaining receivers.

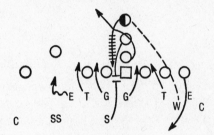

Figure 6-30

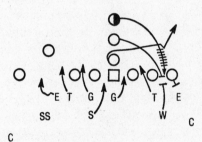

Figure 6-31

CHAPTER 7

UTILIZING THE MULTIPLE DEFENSIVE
PACKAGE TO STOP THE POWER I

The Power I formation has been used successfully by a number of high school and college teams over the past few years. This offense lends itself well to a strong running game because of the alignment of the backs, and with the use of motion by one of the backs the passing game is enhanced.

If a defensive team is physically superior to the offensive personnel, one basic alignment can be used to stop the Power I. Generally, a team that runs the Power I has several big, strong linemen that can drive, can block well, and are able to move the ball on inside plays. The multiple defensive package should help a team that is considerably smaller and less physical up front. The multiple defense should be used to neutralize the physical advantage of the personnel in the Power I by the use of stacks, slants, and movements.

The plays that we feel make up the basic package from the Power I are the isolation of the linebacker, the off-tackle play, the counter option, the sweep, and play action pass plays with one of the backs in motion. There will be variations from team to team, but we must have our personnel positioned in such a way as to provide maximum containment, force, and pursuit on these particular plays.

The alignments and techniques that will be described in this chapter have been used by me at one time or another and have proven successful. These alignments and techniques have been used in both the high school and college ranks. It would be too much to expect from a defensive team to be proficient in all the alignments and stunts, but two or three can be mastered based on the plays you must stop. These alignments and techniques must be worked on the week preceding the game, and the players should know the correct reaction on each alignment against the plays mentioned earlier. A coach should never leave a doubt in a player's mind about his reaction on a particular play.

50 CROSS (See Figure 7-1)

This call is always in our game play against a team that runs from the Power I formation. The cross stunt will be played as explained in Chapter 2, Figure 2-11. The keys for both linebackers should be the near back and the flow. If the ball moves to Sam's side, he shuffles to the outside of his tackle as he reads the play. The linebacker knows that the tackle to his side is coming hard to the inside gap, so if this area is threatened he does not have to step up and take on the block of the guard as he does in a regular 50 Defense. He must shuffle laterally to the outside, keeping his normal depth, and be prepared to protect the area on the outside of the tackle. The linebacker should never overrun the ball.

In Figure 7-1, the Cross is shown against the option to the split end side. If the linebacker reads the play perfectly, he will begin the shuffle as the flow comes to his side, read the ball being pulled from the fullback, and scrape to take the quarterback. If the ball is given to the dive back, the linebacker must step up and close the seam between himself and defensive tackle. This is an excellent call against almost any type of option play since it will sometimes allow the end to come off on the pitch man. The linebacker away from the flow plays 50.

In Figure 7-2, the isolation play is shown. The linebacker must shuffle as he reads the flow and step up to take on the block from the

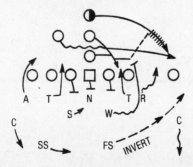

Figure 7-1

near back. The fullback should be caught up inside and should not be able to double team the linebacker as he would in Base 50. The defensive end must work across the face of the tight end once he reads a turnout block. One major coaching point for the linebacker is to never overrun the ball as he shuffles to the outside of the tackle.

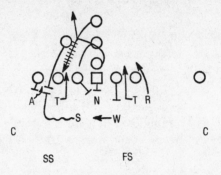

Figure 7-2

50 STRONG SLANT-STAY (See Figure 7-3)

This call is effective against the Power I because it will give the linebacker away-from-the-formation-side help on the isolation play. This call will also allow the nose guard to gain a step on the center if the sweep is run to the strong side of the formation as shown in Figure 7-3. The linebacker away from the strong side should play the same technique as described for the cross stunt. The strong side linebacker must play Base 50 defense but should also be aware that he should receive help from the nose guard if the ball threatens his side.

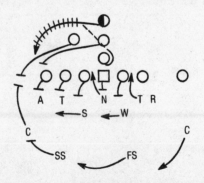

Figure 7-3

If the fullback runs a quick dive play or a cutback play designed to hit over the weak side guard, the linebacker to that side must step up and fill the void between the nose guard and slant tackle as shown in Figure 7-4. Each linebacker must know what the three interior linemen are doing on each stunt so they can either fill or scrape. The secondary will play 1 coverage when the Strong Slant-Stay is called.

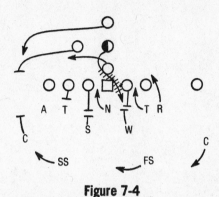

Figure 7-4

50 GAP-OPEN SLANT (See Figure 7-5)

The use of this call gives the defense a great deal of strength to the split end side. The use of the 50 Gap-Open Slant will also help on the isolation to the tight end side, and if moved into at the precise moment it should confuse the blocking pattern of the offensive linemen. This defensive call should also be very effective against the isolation option that a number of Power I teams use. The Willie linebacker must use the technique that was described for the cross stunt as the flow comes to

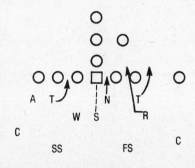

Figure 7-5

him. Once the ball is pulled and the quarterback comes down the line on the option, the Willie linebacker should attack him quickly. This should force an exceptionally quick pitch to the trail back and allow the defense to react to the point of attack. (See Figure 7-6.)

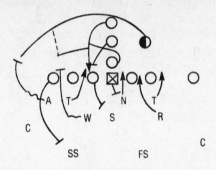

Figure 7-6

One important aspect for you to consider when using this stunt is the swap of assignments by the open side end and tackle. From week to week this may vary. If the offense has a good passing attack, a coach may want maximum pass coverage, which would require the defensive tackle to play his regular 5 technique and the end to drop to the curl on pass action. (See Figure 7-7.) When the X stunt is used with this alignment, the linebackers must take the curl areas if a drop back pass occurs. (See Figure 7-8.)

Anchor—Play a 9 technique to the tight end side.

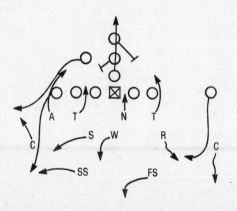

Figure 7-7

Rover—Play a drop technique to the split end and execute an X stunt on the snap.

Open Side Tackle—(split end side) Use a slant technique to the outside and contain.

Closed Side Tackle—(tight end side) Use a slant technique to the inside.

Nose Guard—Play a 1 technique to the split end side.

Sam—Assume a position three yards deep and head on the center. You will key the near back.

Willie—Play your regular 5 technique.

Secondary—Play 1 coverage.

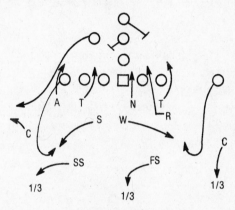

Figure 7-8

THE 53 STACK-DOWN RUSH (See Figure 7-9)

This alignment gives the impression of being a completely new defense, but only the techniques of two positions are different from those of the 53 Stack. The nose guard and Willie linebacker must learn a 1 technique, which is very simple. We tell these two players to slide to the guard center gaps and try to penetrate. They are responsible for stopping the quarterback sneak. The extremely low goal line charge is not used here since we feel we will lose some pursuit, but we do want the players low enough to take on a double team block from the center and guard.

The Sam linebacker must go to the tight end side and execute a stunt between the offensive guard-tackle gap. The strong safety does the same to the split-end side of formation. The defensive tackles slant to the outside and read the flow of the ball. If the flow is to them, they contain. The ends key the tailback, and if he runs a flare route the end to that side must pick him up man to man.

We will utilize this defense whenever an offense takes extremely large splits. We will also use this call against a team that runs many power plays inside. This defense can provide an exceptional pass rush if the Sam linebacker can shift the personnel at the correct time. The responsibilities for this defense and 53 Stack Rush are identical, with the exception of those of the nose guard and the Willie linebacker. The secondary will play man for man coverage when this stunt is called. This call gives the defense a player in each gap once the ball is snapped. If the linebacker and strong safety do not tip the stunts, one or both will come free.

This defense is called 53 Stack-Down because once our players are taught the 53 Stack it is a simple matter to add the word "down" and give a completely new look to the offense. The 53 Stack-Down can be used with nine players, using the techniques learned earlier. Only the nose guard and Willie linebacker have anything new to learn if we want to play the 53 Stack-Down as a read defense.

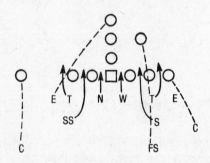

Figure 7-9

THE 70 VERSUS THE POWER I (See Figure 7-10)

The 70 Defense is very effective against an open formation. Whenever a Power I team features a split end, we will use the 70 defense several times a game. How much this call is used will be determined by the opponent's tendency to run to the tight end side and the type of plays and blocking patterns they use.

If, for example, the offense has a sweep they like to run to the ight end side and the onside guard pulls, we would use 70. This call would eliminate the pulling guard because he is now covered or the offense would have to make adjustments in their blocking pattern. The 70 would also provide your linebacker with the freedom to help in he area between the end and tackle since we feel this is the spot where he sweep can hurt a defense the worst. When you have your best linemen on the center's nose, the offense is forced to double team him and the defense loses a big play man. In the 70 Defense, the offense cannot double team the nose guard and you regain the possibility of a big play from your best defensive lineman. The secondary can play either 1 or 2 coverage against this formation when we call 70. (See Figure 7-10.)

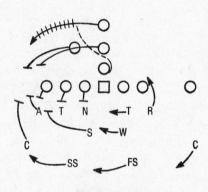

Figure 7-10

70 BINGO (See Figure 7-11)

The Bingo Stunt from the 70 Defense has proven very effective against the Power I counter plays, sweeps, and almost any type of option play to the tight end side of the formation. The Sam linebacker should move the defense from base 50 to 70 and execute the Bingo Stunt on the snap of the ball. Sam must be aware of the area inside of he slanting nose guard. Sam cannot afford to fly to the outside until he is absolutely sure the ball does not threaten the middle.

The tackle to the side of the tight end executes a slant to the outside. The nose guard slants to the tight end side and reads the block of the guard. If the guard reaches the nose guard he should continue his slant. If the guard tries to block the nose guard to the outside, he should run around the block and close down to the ball.

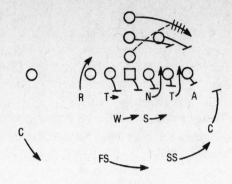

Figure 7-11

70 OPEN DART (See Figure 7-12)

The Open Dart call from a 70 alignment accomplishes what we feel are two very important objectives. First, it will force an offensive center to release to the onside gap when a play is run to the tight end side because he never knows when the nose guard will be stunting. Second, it will allow the Sam linebacker to read the play without having to take on a blocker. Sam should be able to recognize the play and get to the ball much quicker. This call also gives your best lineman a chance to get a jump on the offensive blocker and provide the defense with a big play. The nose guard executes a dart to the guard-center gap, feeling the flow of the ball as he goes. If the flow is to the side of the dart, he clears the gap and looks for the ball. If the flow is away, he runs around the guard and pursues.

80 STRONG SLANT (See Figure 7-13)

The 80 Defense will be used against the Power I formation to force quick assignment changes by the offensive linemen and to keep the quarterback off balance in his play selections. The 80 will be used with a variety of stunts, because to use it as a straight defense would invite a steady diet of big splits by the offensive line and isolation plays in the middle.

The 80 Defense can easily be shifted into from any one of the following alignments: 40, 50 and 53 Stack. It is a good idea to move into the 80 from all three alignments during the course of a game since this adds to the concealment of the primary defense.

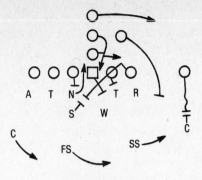

Figure 7-12

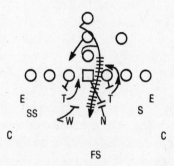

Figure 7-13

The defensive tackles should align themselves in their normal 80 techniques. On the snap of the ball, the tackle to the strong side of the formation must take a short lateral step with the outside foot and anticipate the offensive tackle blocking down. As the tackle steps, he should keep his eyes to the inside to determine the flow. If the flow is to him, he must work through the tackle's block. If the flow is away from him, he must run around the guard and pursue. The backside tackle executes a slant to the inside and reads as he goes to the guard-center gap. If the flow is to the strong side, he must flatten to the line of scrimmage and pursue. If flow is to the weak side, the tackle must run around the guard's block.

The 80 Defense can be played against a two tight-end formation and is balanced to both sides. We will use the strong slant to the strength of the formation. The back who is in the position of a halfback determines the strength of the Power I. This call is very effective against traps, isolations, and the counter plays that are run from this formation. The 80 Strong Slant is run with either man coverage or three deep zone coverage by the secondary. When the offense is in a two tight end formation, we use a 3 call. If a split end is employed by the offense, we will use man coverage.

80 DOWN (See Figure 7-14)

This defense is as old as the game of football itself. We refer to it as 80 Down, but is commonly called a Gap 8.

We will use this defense on a definite running down when the offense tendencies indicate an inside running play. The alignment prior to the snap of the ball is the normal 80, but as the quarterback goes into his cadence, the Sam linebacker will give a command of "move" and the linebackers will move to the near gap and assume a three-point stance. The technique of each player in a gap is very simple. On the snap of the ball, penetrate the line of scrimmage staying as low as possible; find the ball; pursue.

This defense is used on short yardage situations and against certain blocking patterns. The 80 Down can also provide a great pass rush. The secondary coverage will be in man for man, with the end to the strong side checking the fullback.

A few years ago I had the pleasure of participating in the Sugar Bowl as an assistant coach. Our opponent had an excellent football team that featured an outstanding passer. At one point in the season, they held the number one spot in the AP and UPI polls. As was expected, both teams scored several points and the momentum would swing first one way and then the other. Late in the fourth quarter, with our defense on the field and clinging to a six point lead, we felt it was

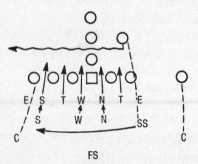

Figure 7-14

time to take a calculated risk. The situation was third and nine on our own forty-five yard line, with just over two and a half minutes to play. We called the 80 Down, got a great rush on the quarterback which caused him to throw off balance, and our free safety intercepted the pass. Our offense ground out two first downs, and we won the game. This was the only time we used this particular defense in the game.

80 PINCH (See Figure 7-15)

The 80 Pinch has been a very good call against the Power I formation that features a strong inside running game. This call is also excellent against the offense in short yardage situations and all types of option plays. The secondary will play 1 coverage against a split end formation and 3 coverage against two tight ends. The assignments for each position are as follows:

Anchor End—Line up in a 9 technique if you are playing against a tight end and come underneath him on the snap. If the option shows, take the quarterback. If you have a split end to your side, play a standup 5 technique and come down off the hip of the offensive tackle. You still have the quarterback on the option.

Rover—Your alignments are the same as those of the anchor.

Strong Tackle—Line up in a 3 technique and fire the guard-center gap on movement of the ball.

Weak Tackle—You have the same responsibilities as the strong tackle.

Nose Guard—Play a standup 1 technique to the strong side or tight end side. Key the quarterback. If the flow is to your side scrape around your slant tackle and fill the guard-tackle gap. If the flow is away from you, play your regular 80 technique.

Willie—Play this stunt exactly as described for the nose guard.

Sam—Play a standup 7 technique. Key near the back and the ball. If the flow is to you, scrape outside for the pitch on the option. If a sweep action shows, you must contain the play. If the ball goes away from you, work behind the line of scrimmage, alert for play action passes and reserves.

Strong Safety—If the offense has a formation with a split end, you will go to the split end side and take your alignment in 1 swap coverage. If the offense has a closed formation, you will go the weak side and play a standup 7 technique. When in the 7 technique, you must read the near back and the flow of the ball. If the flow is to you, scrape outside to contain. If the flow is away from you get depth as you work behind the line of scrimmage looking for reverses and play action passes.

Cornerbacks—Play either 3 or 1 Swap coverage, depending on the formation.

Free Safety—You are responsible for recognizing the formation and calling out the correct coverage.

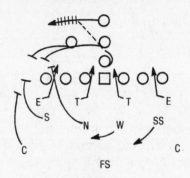

Figure 7-15

80 SLIDE (See Figure 7-16)

This alignment is similar to the 80 Down since it is a gap-type defense to the strong side of the formation. The difference is in the alignment and play of the Willie linebacker. This call can provide a maximum pass rush, with all eligible receivers covered, and can be used extensively against the Power I in short yardage situations and as a change-up goal line defense. The defense should move from the 80 alignment to the 80 Slide.

The Sam linebacker's technique is the same as it was in the 80 Down. The Willie linebacker must key the flow of the ball and play his normal standup 1 technique. If the flow comes to Willie's side, he must be alert to fill the gap between the nose guard who is slanting to the tight end side and the 3 technique.

The techniques for each position in the 80 Slide will not be discussed against the Power I. If you wish, refer to Chapter 5 for a brief review of this defensive alignment.

The secondary will play man coverage when 80 Slide is called.

The free safety should be aligned over the football, eight yards deep. If the triple option is run from this formation, the free safety should take the pitch to both sides of the formation. (See Figures 7-17 and 7-18.)

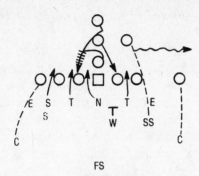

Figure 7-16

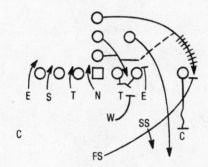

Figure 7-17

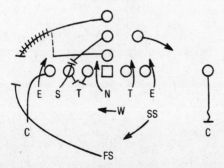

Figure 7-18

GOAL LINE DEFENSES AND THE POWER I

The Power I formation is a favorite goal line formation for many high school and college teams. This is because of the strong running game that is so necessary when the offense is operating within a limited area on the field.

When we face a Power I team, we want to be sure that our personnel is placed in a position to counter the running game and take away the pass. Our linebackers must align themselves according to the backfield set. For instance, in the 60 Defense if our linebackers see a balanced set such as a pro formation with split backs or I, they would line up over the outside shoulders of the offensive guards. (See Figure 7-19.) If the offense shows a three back set such as the Wishbone or Power I and 60 Defense is called, we feel there must be a middle linebacker. (See Figure 7-20.)

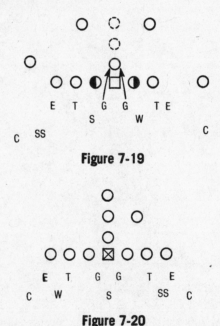

Figure 7-19

Figure 7-20

Once we go to the middle linebacker scheme against a three back set, we must teach our Willie linebacker and strong safety combo coverage. Combo coverage means that the strong safety and Willie Linebacker play the ends to their sides man to man. The cornerbacks are the contain portion of the defense and take the pitch on all options. In Figure 7-21, an option is shown against the 60 Defense. In Figure 7-22, a play action pass is shown.

Once the strong safety knows the end is blocking, he can concentrate on the running play. If he is unsure, he must play the pass. In Figure 7-22, the end is releasing and the strong safety must take him on whatever route he runs.

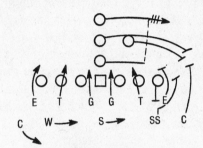

Figure 7-21

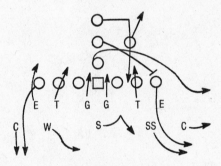

Figure 7-22

60 BLITZ (See Figure 7-23)

The 60 Blitz that we run against a three back set such as the Power I would differ from the 60 Blitz as described in Chapter 6 against the Slot I. The assignments for the Sam linebacker and strong safety would change, and, of course, there would be no combo coverage.

Ends—Play 60 Blitz. Take the back who flares out to your side.

Tackles—Play 60 Blitz. Slant outside and find the ball.

Guards—Play your 1 technique as described in Chapter 6.

Sam—Align over the ball at a depth at which you can clear the defensive tackles' feet. Key the quarterback. You must go with the ball and close off all seams between the defensive tackles.

  Willie—Align at a depth of one yard off the line of scrimmage and slightly on the outside of your defensive tackle. On the snap of the ball, hit the offensive guard-tackle gap. Timing is very important, so watch the movement of the ball.

  Strong Safety—Align to the strong side of the formation a yard off the line of scrimmage and slightly outside of your defensive tackle. On the snap of the ball, hit the guard-center gap and be ready to meet a lead blocker.

  Cornerbacks—Key the end to your side. If he releases on a pass route, cover him. If he blocks, you can help on the run.

  The 60 Blitz that we use against the Power I and Wishbone is very effective when a team attempts to block your middle linebacker with one of the guards. Most of the time the stunting linebacker or strong safety will come free as shown in Figure 7-23.

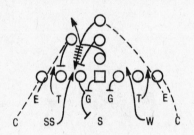

Figure 7-23

60 STACK PINCH (Figure 7-24)

  Once the goal line attack pattern has been established and we feel certain the Power I team is going to run inside, we use the 60 Stack Pinch. This call puts a defensive lineman in each gap and should free the Sam linebacker to meet a back who attempts to jump over the pile. This alignment is also very confusing to the offensive lineman if used in conjunction with your regular 60 alignment. We attempt to make something happen with this defense.

  Ends—Align in a tight 9 technique. On the snap, come inside the tight end. Attempt to penetrate to a point one yard deep in the backfield.

  Tackles—Align in a head up position on the offensive tackle. On the snap of the ball, come down hard to the inside gap. Don't be turned to the outside.

Strong Side Guard—On the linebacker's command, move to a head up position on the offensive guard. On the snap, slant to the inside gap. You should attempt to go for the quarterback's foot that is nearest to your.

Weak Side Guard—Slide to a head up position on the center and slant to the weak side gap when the ball moves. You must stay low and penetrate.

Sam—Align behind the weak side guard and key the ball. Be ready for a back jumping over the linemen.

Willie—Align on the inside shoulder of the tight end to your side. Play a combo coverage with your cornerback. If the tight end blocks, you can check for the run.

Strong Safety—Same techniques as described for the Willie linebacker.

Cornerbacks—Play a combo coverage. Key the back nearest to you.

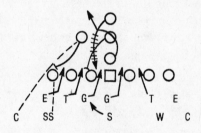

Figure 7-24

CHAPTER 8

DEFENDING THE PASSING GAME
WITH THE MULTIPLE THEME

In the past several years, the passing game in high school and college football has become highly sophisticated due to the influence of the professional teams. It is not surprising to see a high school team throw the ball twenty to thirty times per game. Several years ago, this would have been something out of the ordinary.

When setting up a game plan against a team that relies a great deal upon the passing attack, we want to know certain factors. These factors will influence each defensive call we make in a game.

1. What physical and emotional qualities does the opposing quarterback possess? (Is he a true drop back passer or a scrambler? Does he retain his poise under pressure?)

2. Which receiver is the most prolific, and which receiver does the quarterback favor in "make" or "break" situations?

3. We must know what type of pass blocking scheme our opponents will employ since this will determine the type of rush we must use to get to the passer.

4. The defense must be aware of the types of passes that will be used from each formation; e.g., drop back passes from the split backs formation, sprint out passes from the I, and so on.

5. Our defensive unit must know the favorite pass routes and the passes used in certain areas of the field. Some teams will have certain passes for each zone of the field.

6. We must know if the quarterback can check off at the line of scrimmage against certain defenses. If we show a loaded front

and he checks off, we must be able to move from this front back into a base defense. For example, it is sometimes very confusing to the quarterback if we line up in a 50 Stack and shift to Base 50.

After we gather the data we feel is pertinent, we will compile the information and make a decision as to the direction we will go in defending against this attack. We want our game plan to be based on concrete conclusions of what we must do on defense in order to nullify the opponent's passing game. We want to be able to defend against the passing game in several ways. We want the quarterback to read our coverage after the snap and not prior to the snap. In the following paragraphs, the reader will see that we can rush from three to eight players, thereby keeping the offensive line and quarterback unsure of blocking rules and the types of coverage that will be employed.

THE 50 ROVER-GAP (See Figure 8-1)

The 50 Defense, as we use it, is a five-man line against the run and a four-man line against the pass. We feel this defense combines the advantages of both schemes. Since we will play the Base 50 against all formations, we must be able to play good pass defense in any situation.

The Rover-Gap call is used when we discover that our opponents use what we refer to as turn-out pass blocking, which occurs when the offensive guards drop back and block the defensive tackles, the offensive tackles block the ends, and the center blocks the nose guard. The running backs must check the linebackers for a blitz and then run a pass route if the backers drop to a zone.

The nose guard will line up in a 0 technique, and on the command

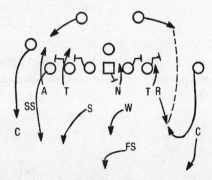

Figure 8-1

of "move" he will shift to the guard-center gap toward the rover end. From this alignment, it is almost impossible for a center to block the nose guard by himself if the nose guard moves on the snap. When the Rover-Gap is used, the entire offensive line to this side is affected and the blocking scheme must be adjusted. The turn-out blocking scheme is shown along with the Rover-Gap in Figure 8-1. This call in no way affects the play of the defensive linemen or secondary. The linebacker to the rover side must compensate by stacking behind the nose guard. The Rover-Gap should help free the linebacker if a running play develops.

50 WALK (See Figure 8-2)

This call is used in a definite throwing situation against a pro formation when we feel the offense will try to get the ball to the split end on a quick route. The routes we try to eliminate are the quick post, the quick screen, and the short out pattern.

The rover end will align himself in his usual drop technique against a pro formation. Once the quarterback goes into his cadence, the rover will move out to a position two yards inside the split end and four yards off the line of scrimmage. We want a two yard cushion between the rover and the split end to protect against the quick post. The rover should assume a stance with his outisde foot back and his body opened toward the split end. The rover should read the quarterback's action and feel the release of the end. If the end tries to release in an inside route, the rover should deliver a blow and give ground. If the end takes an abnormal split, the rover must not go all the way out but adjust himself to the field. If a drop back pass occurs, Rover will give ground and squeeze the curl area while checking the near back for a flare pattern.

The secondary will play I Invert Coverage with a slight technique change for the free safety. Whereas the free safety had to contain and take the pitch on I Invert coverage if the flow showed to the split end side, he now must support just outside the weak tackle and take the quarterback on the option. The rover end will now be the contain portion of the defense and take the pitch. A lot of teams will automatically run the option to the split end side once the end shows the walk-off position. We have found the technique that has just been described very effective against this type of attack. (See Figure 8-3.)

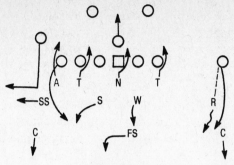

Figure 8-2

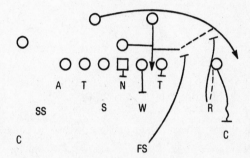

Figure 8-3

50 STRONG SLANT (See Figure 8-4.)

The Strong Slant was described in Chapter 1. We want to use the Strong Slant for two primary reasons: to help on the option pass to the tight end in the seam, and to give a change-up on the pass rush.

Against a drop back attack, the strong slant will confuse the quarterback if he attempts to read the underneath coverage of the linebackers and rover end.

In Base 50, the Sam linebacker must go to the strong side curl, Willie to the middle, and the rover to the weak curl. In the Strong Slant, the end to the strong side takes the curl as Sam covers the middle and Willie goes to the weak side curl. The rover end has to rush the passer.

This call should also present problems to the offensive linemen if they anticipate the rover end dropping off into pass coverage and he rushes to passer. A number of teams will double team the nose guard with the center and weak guard and block the offensive tackle on the defensive 5 technique to the rover end's side. This blocking scheme will leave the rover free to put tremendous pressure on the quarterback.

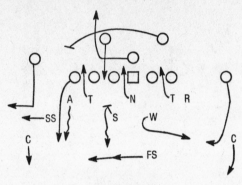

Figure 8-4

50 PREVENT (See Figure 8-5)

The 50 Prevent that we utilize at Mississippi State can be used in any situation because we will play Base 50 against the run and 50 Prevent against a straightback pass. This defense is played as a key defense by the entire unit. In other words, we play 50 Prevent only when the quarterback drops back to throw. Other actions are played using basic 50 techniques. This call will allow us to get an extra man into the underneath pass coverage, which should eliminate the short passing game.

In Figure 8-6, a running play is shown against the 50 Prevent. Everyone must play his normal techniques until the pass develops. When a drop back pass shows, we go to our responsibilities in the 50 Prevent.

The responsibilities for each position are as follows:

Anchor—Play 50. If a drop back pass occurs, you must take the curl area as you would in a Strong Slant.

Rover—Play 50. Work the curl and key the near back.

Strong T.—Play 50. If a drop back pass shows, contain the rush.

Weak T.—Same as strong tackle.

Nose—Play 50.

Sam—Play 50. If a drop back pass occurs, you have a strong middle hook.

Will—Play 50. If a drop back pass occurs, you have the weak middle hook.

Secondary—Play 1 coverage or 3 coverage.

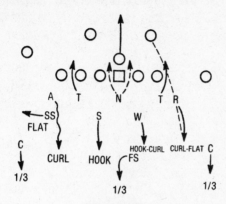

Figure 8-5

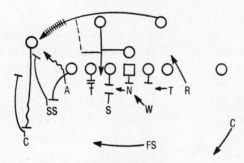

Figure 8-6

50 RUSH (See Figure 8-7)

The blitz from the 50 Defense has been very effective for us in the past few years. We feel that for a rush to be effective it should be run from the defense that is used most of the time in passing situations. We want our linebackers to remain at the depth they usually play and not to tip the rush. We also do not want the secondary to cheat up too quickly and show the man to man coverage. We want the offense to feel as if we are going to play Base 50 Defense.

We want to cover all five receivers and rush six or seven people. In order to cover all eligible receivers, we must use either a linebacker or an end. We prefer to use an end and fire the linebackers. This rush has proven to be very effective against a drop back pass and a sprint out attack to the strong side. If the offense does not run a back out to the strong side, the defense has the tackle and end to pull up the quarterback very quickly. Before the end comes up to contain, he must be absolutely sure that there is no back coming out to the strong side. In Figure 8-7, the 50 Rush is shown against I with the sprint, and generally there is no threat of a back getting out from this formation. The anchor end should move back off the line of scrimmage on the snap and read the plas. If there is no threat of a third receiver to his side, he can rush the passer.

Nose—Execute a strong dart.

Sam—Fire the strong side tackle-guard gap.

Will—Fire the weak side guard-center gap.

S.T.—Execute slant out technique. Contain rush.

W.T.—Execute slant out technique. Contain rush.

Anchor—Spy; take the fullback if he flares.

Rover—Execute an X stunt.

S.S.—Play man coverage.

F.S.—Play man coverage.

S.C.—Play man coverage.

W.C.—Play man coverage.

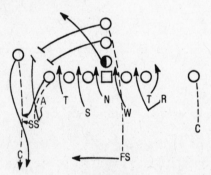

Figure 8-7

53 STACK PREVENT (See Figure 8-8)

This call can present quite a problem to the quarterback since he is anticipating a rush from this alignment but, instead, the defense will drop eight people on pass coverage. With the threat of several different ways to put pressure on the passer, namely by rushing four, five, six, or if the coach has the nerve, eight players, the quarterback is thinking about releasing the ball to his primary receiver quickly. The offensive linemen are also thinking about blocking the different stunts that can take place, and if the noseguard and tackles can get a good jump on the blockers they should be able to put a certain amount of pressure on the passer. This defense gives excellent underneath coverage but is somewhat vulnerable to the sideline or quick out routes by the wide receivers. In order to cover this weakness, the free safety and cornerbacks should fake man to man coverage and then move back to their positions in the 3 coverage. (See Figure 8-9.)

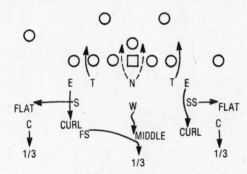

Figure 8-8

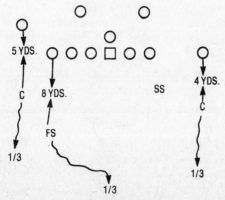

Figure 8-9

40 DEFENSE WITH STRONG-WEAK COMBO

The combo calls were described in Chapter 1 and Chapter 2. We will play the 40 Defense with a combo call a great deal in passing situations, especially if our opponent has an exceptional wide receiver and the passer drops straight back. This allows us to play him tough on the short routes with a cornerback and still have help against the deep patterns. This call is used in third and six or more situations when the offensive tendency is to get the ball to their favorite receiver. We still have all remaining zones covered, with the linebackers working away from the combo call. The 40 Defense, using the Combo Strong or Weak, is one of our favorite calls against a pure drop back team. Combo calls can only be used against a pro formation. If a slot formation is shown by the offense, the free safety must make sure the coverage is checked to 1. (See Figure 8-10.)

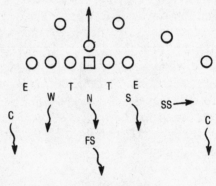

Figure 8-10

The cornerback to the side of the combo call should attempt to make the coverage look as muck like 2 coverage as possible. On the snap of the ball, the defensive back should retreat four to five steps and read the release of the wide receiver. Most receivers have a certain release from the line of scrimmage for each route to be run. The corner hangs tough on any routes up to twelve yards deep, and at the same time he must be reading the release of the tight end or second inside receiver. If the second receiver breaks to the flat, the corner must come off the wide receiver and pick up the man in the flat. This coverage is great against a quick out cut or short curl by the receiver to the side of the call. (See Figure 8-11.)

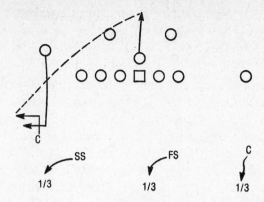

Figure 8-11

EAGLE SLANT

We attempt to run an Eagle look to the split end side of formation for two reasons. First, we run it to give help on the inside run game to the split end side of formation. With the defensive tackle in a 3 technique on the offensive guard, it should take some pressure off the linebacker to that side when a team is running the isolation play and base blocking the 50. Second, the Eagle alignment should also help to confuse the quarterback's read when the offense is running the Veer to the split end side because the quarterback is not sure who has the dive on each play since the end and linebacker to that side can change responsibilities. (See Figure 8-12.)

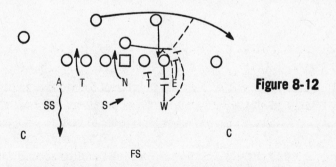

Figure 8-12

We also use the Eagle Slant to give a change-up on our pass coverage since most Eagle alignments only use two players in underneath pass coverage. Generally, the two linebackers have to play curl coverage, which leaves the middle open for a crossing receiver or a delay route by one of the running backs. (See Figure 8-13.)

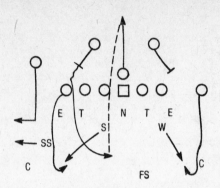

Figure 8-13

In order to alleviate this problem, we use the Eagle Slant to entice the offense to throw in the middle or pick on our underneath coverage. The Eagle Slant is a combination of the Weak and Strong Slants. There are a couple of adjustments that have to be made. One, we will always slant to the tight end side of formation. (See Figure 8-14.) Two, the Eagle tackle (3 technique) does not have to slant because he is already lined up in the position that he would be if he lined up in a 5 technique and slanted inside. This tackle plays a read 3 technique. (See Figure 8-15.)

The technique for the Sam linebacker is the same in the Strong Slant when facing a pro formation. If the near back dives, he must fill

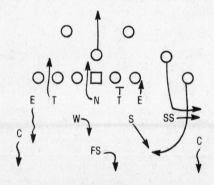

Figure 8-14

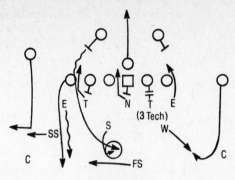

Figure 8-15

inside his tackle. In a drop back pass, Sam must take all drag or delay routes by the tight end or backs. (See Figure 8-15.)

EAGLE RUSH

Holding true to our philosophy of playing technique defense and pressure defense from the same alignment, we use the Eagle Rush to cause something to happen. The Eagle Rush is used in situations in which an inside run play or a drop back pass is anticipated.

The Eagle Rush has been very effective as a pass rush because of the overload in the middle of the offensive line. The only player who should be able to pick up the stunting linebacker is one of the two running backs. When facing a team that features the rollout pass from the pro-set, the Willie linebacker should come free, and as the defensive end pulls up the quarterback he must make the play from the backside. (See Figure 8-16.)

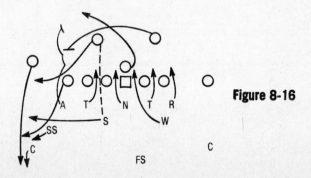

Figure 8-16

The assignments and responsibilities for each player in the Eagle Rush are outlined as follows:

Anchor End—Play a 9 technique to the tight end side of formation.

Rover End—Play a loose 5 technique to the split end side of the formation.

Tackle to the tight end side—If the strong side is to you, execute a slant to the inside. If the strength of the formation is away from you and you have a tight end to your side, you must play technique because of the seam that develops between you and the defensive end if you go to the inside.

Split end side tackle—Slide down to a 3 technique on the guard, and on the snap of the ball come upfield. Don't read; get penetration and look for the ball.

Sam—You must go to the strong side of the formation and pick up the third receiver man to man.

Willie—Align to the weak side of the offensive formation, and on the snap of the ball run through the guard-center gap to the split end side. Against a pro formation, this is the guard-center gap to the weak side. Against a slot formation, this is the guard-center gap to the strong side.

Nose—Execute a dart to the tight end side of the formation.

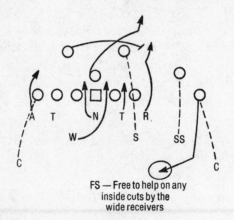

FS — Free to help on any
inside cuts by the
wide receivers

Figure 8-17

Secondary—The secondary must play man coverage. The corners have the wide outs man to man, with the strong safety taking the second receiver to the strong side. The free safety must take the back to the weak side of the formation. Against a Slot formation, the weak safety should become free at times to help on the wide receivers. This is especially true if a rollout pass is run and the offense brings the weak back across to block the end as shown in Figure 8-17.

CHAPTER 9

DEFENDING UNUSUAL FORMATIONS
WITH BASIC DEFENSES

Prior to the start of a season, every defensive coaching staff should discuss unusual offensive formations and how they will be defended. There should be certain rules formulated for the defensive signal callers and for each position. There is nothing so frustrating as an offense that throws a "junk" formation at the defense and picks up good yardage after being shut down most of the game.

We have a few rules for our people on defense that should be effective against any type of spread or "junk" formation. These rules are given out and worked on during early fall practice. During the season, we must brush up on these rules in order to be ready for spreads and/or unusual formations. These rules will stand up in most instances. (See Figures 9-1, 9-2, and 9-3.)

Anchor—If three players split wide, go with them and play a 9 technique on the end. If all three are backs, play over the third man three yards off the line.

Rover—Go to a walk position with two wide men when you hear the call "spread."

Tackles—If the offensive tackle splits out, move to a 3 technique on the guard. Your rush lanes are outside.

Nose—Play a regular 0 technique unless you hear "Check 40."

Sam—Call "Spread" once the offense shows the "junk" formation. If four players have split wide, move your tackle to a 3 technique and go outside to a position that will allow you to play pass and help on the run to the overloaded side.

Willie—You play a regular 3 technique unless four players are split wide, in which case you play head up and four yards deep on the second player from the inside.

Strong Safety—Play a 3 call. You take the strong side flat. Play head up and six yards deep on the second player from the outside.

Cornerbacks—Play a 3 call.

Free Safety—Check the coverage called in the huddle to 3. Make absolutely sure that all four defenders in the secondary get the call.

The rules that were previously discussed are used when we are in our basic 50 Defense and are carried into every game. If we have seen a team use a "junk" formation, we may decide to check to a different defense or a "special" call for that particular opponent.

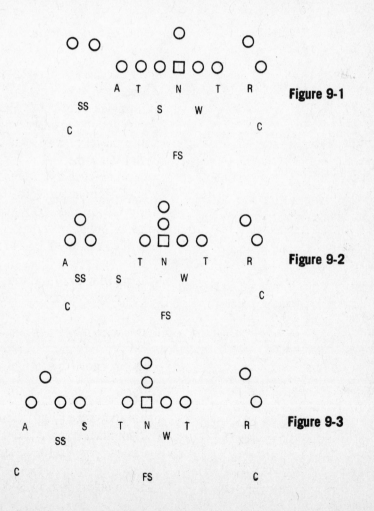

Figure 9-1

Figure 9-2

Figure 9-3

CHECKING DEFENSES

Frequently during the course of a season our defensive unit must be able to move smoothly from one defense to another in order to place strength against strength. In order to accomplish this objective, the entire unit must watch the offense as they break the huddle and be alert for the check by the Sam linebacker. For instance, if the 40 Defense has been built into the game plan during the week against a certain formation. Sam should shout "Check 40, Check 40" once this particular formation is shown. (See Figure 9-4.) The call in the huddle is 50, but when the offense shifts to the spread the defense is checked and moves to the 40.

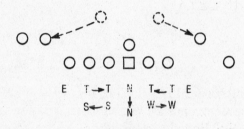

Figure 9-4

Another example of a call that has considerable merit is the 50 Strong Slant against a team that uses strong motion and throws the pullup pass series to the strong side. The defense is placing strength against strength and also getting a good pass rush on the quarterback from the backside. (See Figure 9-5.) This call is used whenever the defense gets this formation and the tailback motions to the strong side.

One year I had the pleasure of working with a fine group of young men who beat L.S.U. in Tiger Stadium at Baton Rouge 16-7. L.S.U. ran two pass patterns from the Slot I formation that had been very successful for them in three previous games. Our defensive staff felt that if we could stop these two patterns we would have an excellent chance of winning the game. Both of these pass plays came from the Slot I formation, with motion by the tailback to the strong side.

Our defensive staff decided to play a Strong Slant each time L.S.U. gave tailback motion to the strong side. In order to let our linemen know which way to slant, the Sam linebacker would call out "Bingo, right" or "Bingo, left." The free safety would check from 1 coverage to a strong zone call that would allow both the strong safety and strong cornerback to play the short routes of the split end and slotback very tough.

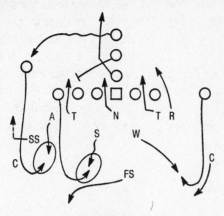

Figure 9-5

In the strong zone call, the free safety moves to a position from which he can cover the outside receiver deep if he runs a streak as shown in Figure 9-6. Both the strong corner and the strong safety read the route of the second receiver. If the inside receiver runs an out cut, the strong safety can work slowly back to the curl as he checks for a third receiver in the flat. The strong corner can now start back slowly and then come up quickly to stop the out cut. He can play this route

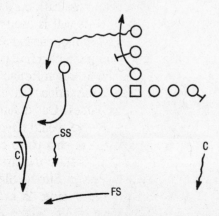

Figure 9-6

very tough and disregard the outside receiver because he knows that the free safety will pick up the deep receiver. (See Figure 9-7.) The strong safety must read the out cut by the slot man as he settles slowly to the curl area. If a third receiver threatens the flat, the strong safety immediately comes up to cover him.

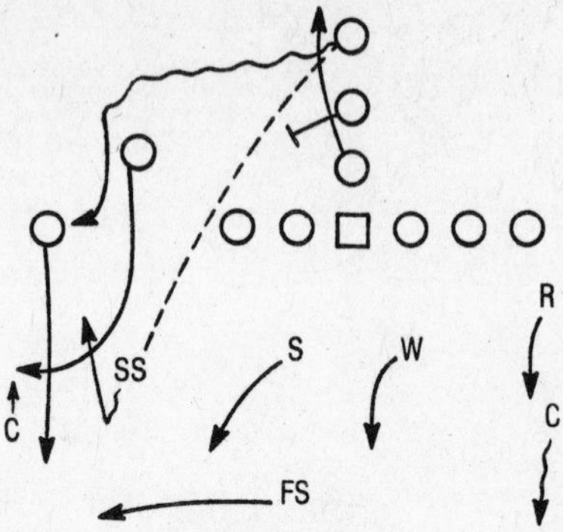

Figure 9-7

The two patterns that we had to stop in order to beat L.S.U. are shown in Figures 9-8 and 9-9. The bingo slant utilizing a strong zone call is also shown. How well this preparation worked is evidenced by the fact that Mississippi State won the game convincingly and our strong corner was voted the A.P. and U.P.I. defensive player of the week in the Southeastern Conference.

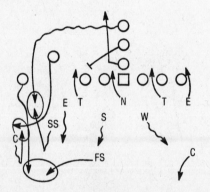

Figure 9-8

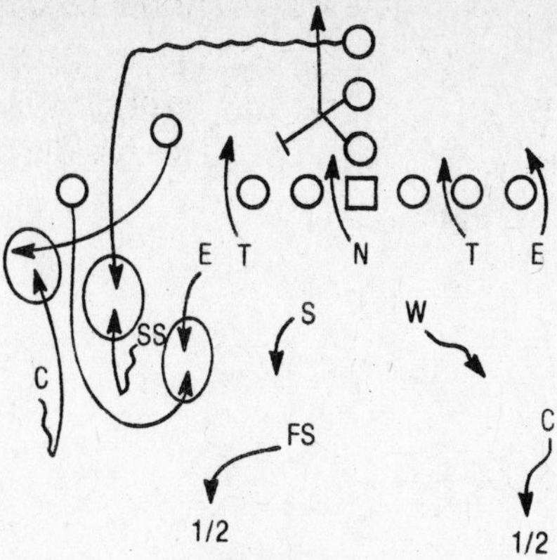

Figure 9-9

50 PREVENT (See Figure 9-10)

We use this defense a great deal just before the end of the first half or at the end of the game. This defense can also be used as a ''surprise defense'' if the offense begins to split all over the field. The ends play their regular techniques until a pass shows, and then they must cover the curl areas. The linebackers play at a depth of five yards and the middle hook zones. The secondary plays a 3 call. The tackles and nose guard play their regular 50 techniques unless the play is a drop back pass, in which case the tackles must rush outside and the nose guard can go to either side.

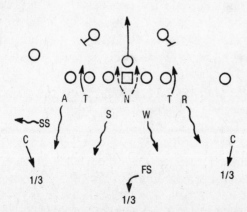

Figure 9-10

If we add the word "walk" to 50 Prevent, it allows the weak side end to walk off on a split receiver to his side. This call should keep the offense from throwing the quick out cut to the split end in order to stop the clock. This call is usually most effective just before half time or the end of the game. (See Figure 9-11.)

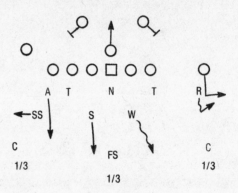

Figure 9-11

53 STACK

There are times during the season when a defense will find itself in a position where they cannot afford to give up any yardage. This is especially true if you are leading by a point or two late in the game, the ball is around midfield, and the opponents have a good field goal kicker. It is my opinion that the quarterback must never be able to tell what the defense is going to do: rush or defend. My personal philosophy is that all five eligible receivers must be covered and pressure applied to the quarterback to make him throw off rhythm. This means rushing six players and covering with five.

The 53 Stack is a valuable defense when you are faced with the above situation. Because of the different combinations that we employ, it is very disconcerting to the offensive signal caller. The calls that are employed are the 53 Stack Rush, the 53 Stack Prevent, and the 53 Stack Rip. (See Chapter 8.) The 53 Stack Prevent can also be used against certain types of spread formations and surprise formations with a few adjustments by the Sam linebacker, ends, and strong safety. (See Figure 9-12.)

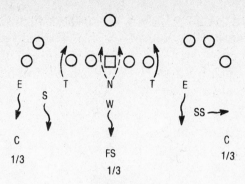

Figure 9-12

THE 40

The 40 Defense is probably the best defense against a spread formation since you have your underneath defenders lined up in their pass zones and you get a good outside rush from your ends.

If we know an opponent has a spread formation, the 40 Defense will be built into the game plan. Only against certain unbalanced sets should the 40 not be used.

A few years ago, while coaching high school football, I had the opportunity to work with a fine group of young men who needed only one victory to win the conference championship. Their opponent was in the same position, and our school had not beaten this team in nineteen years. Our opponents ran primarily from the I and double wing formations. Their quarterback was having a tremendous year, especially in running the sprint-out series from the double wing formation.

We decided to utilize the 50 and 80 Defenses against the I formation and the 40 Defense when our opponents went into the double wing or spread set. We also knew we must contain the quarterback with our ends and apply pressure from underneath. We told our nose guard to rush the quarterback once he read the sprint option. (See Figure 9-13.)

How well this worked was evidenced by the fact that with only two minutes left, the ball around midfield, and our opponents behind by two points, their quarterback ran the sprint-out three straight times. The first pass was incomplete. On the second down, our end did a great job of pulling up the quarterback, and the nose guard tackled him for a five yard loss. On the third down, the quarterback was pressured, he threw off stride, and our cornerback intercepted to assure the victory.

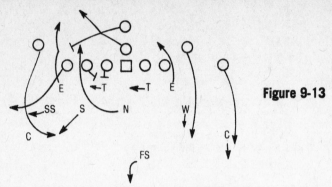

Figure 9-13

80 PREVENT (See Figure 9-14.)

The 80 Prevent is used when the offense is backed up and long yardage must be made on one down. This call gives the defense nine players covering the different zones and two players rushing the quarterback.

The 80 Prevent will be played in the same manner as the 80 against running plays and action passes. If a drop back pass occurs, nine players will defend and two will rush. The assignments for each position are as follows:

Anchor—Play a 9 technique on the left side. If a drop back pass occurs, take the near end.

Rover—Play a 9 technique (standup 5 if you have a split end) on the right side. Take the near curl on a drop back pass.

Tackles—Play a 3 technique and rush to the outside on a straight back pass.

Nose—Play a standup 1 technique and check the near back on passes. Work on the middle hook.

Willie—Play a standup 1. Check the near back on drop back passes. Take the middle area inside the curl zone.

Sam—Play a standup 7 technique and take the flat on drop back passes.

Strong Safety—Play 3 coverage, but play it from a Swap position. You have the flat to your side on drop back action.

Cornerbacks—Play 3 coverage.

Free Safety—Play 3 coverage.

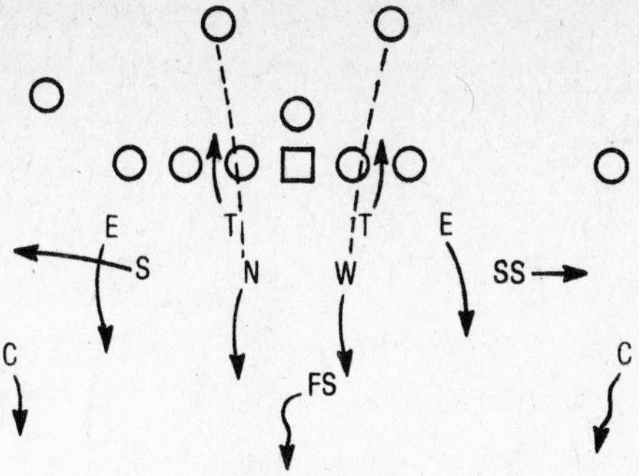

Figure 9-14

GOAL LINE DEFENSES AGAINST UNUSUAL FORMATIONS

Several times during the course of a season, a defense will be faced with several unusual formations on the goal line. These formations are designed to confuse and throw the defense off balance to take advantage of a weak spot.

The formations that we generally see on the goal line that are unusual are the Wishbone with an unbalanced line, an end over with split backs, and a spread formation with one setback. These formations will be defended with our basic 60 defense. Most of the time, we must check out of a rush because of the adjustments that must be made by the front. If we see a certain formation and have practiced against it, we will have a rush ready to run against all formations.

We generally substitute for our nose guard and free safety when the offense gets to our six yard line. (Refer to Chapter 6.) If the situation was third and goal from the six, we would probably leave these two players in the game and play 50 Defense.

UNBALANCED LINE-WISHBONE

Our basic rule against the true unbalanced line is to slide our front one position to the strength of the formation. Against the unbalanced wishbone, we must be alert for the inside belly and sweep to the strong side and the rollout pass to the short side. Generally, the offense tries to break the huddle and run the play on a quick count so as to allow very little time for the defense to recognize the formation and adjust.

The unbalance line with the wishbone set is shown in Figure 9-15.

As mentioned earlier, the front must slide to the strength of the formation. The Sam linebacker should stack behind the tackle nearest the ball in order to help on dive plays to either side.

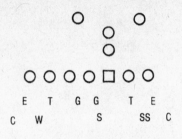

Figure 9-15

END OVER FORMATION (See Figure 9-16)

This formation is designed to confuse the strong safety. Most of the time, the strong safety is keying the tight end and playing him man to man. If the strong safety doesn't realize the tight end is ineligible and switch to the man in the slot, there is one receiver open, as shown in Figure 9-17. The linemen play their regular 60 techniques. The linebackers key the setbacks and play them man for man if they run a pass route.

SPREAD FORMATION (See Figure 9-18)

This formation is usually shifted into from the I set. The purpose of the spread formation is to isolate a fast running back on a linebacker or end. The defensive linemen should play their regular 60 techniques since the linebackers make the adjustments. The Sam linebacker should move over the ball as a middle linebacker and key the quarterback-fullback. The Willie linebacker must move out to cover the back in the slot. We try to put the best pass defender of the two linebackers on the back. This means that at times we have Sam on the back and Willie in the middle.

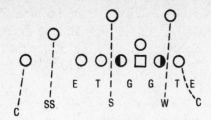

Figure 9-16

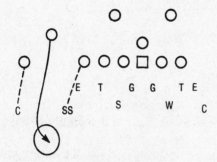

Figure 9-17

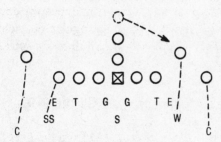

Figure 9-18

CHAPTER 10

USING MULTIPLE DRILLS TO
DEVELOP A HARD-NOSED DEFENSE

The way to teach individual fundamentals and team defense is by making a wise selection of drills and repeating them until the correct response is formed. I believe whatever success a coach enjoys is in direct proportion to his ability to devise and organize the proper drills to meet his particular style of play. The drills that are described in the following pages have been tried and proven effective over the years. You should vary the drills from day to day to avoid monotony, and the drills should not be continued for too long a period of time. If the athletes have a great deal of enthusiasm, they will accomplish the purpose of the drills.

SEVEN CHECKPOINTS FOR DEFENSIVE LINEMEN

There are seven very valuable checkpoints that should be stressed to defensive linemen. The drills that are used to teach fundamentals should take these points into consideration.

(1) *Alignment*—We want a player to align perfectly on each and every play. A lineman can line up a fraction too wide or too tight and weaken the entire defense. This is especially true when the defense moves from one look to another.

(2) *Stance*—All players should be in a position to execute their responsibilities. Regardless of whether a coach believes in the three- or four-point stance, the weight should be equally distributed, with the feet parallel, the back flat, and the head up. The lineman must be able

to move in three directions: right, left, and straight ahead. He should never move backwards.

(3) *Key*—A lineman must be able to locate the point of attack an instant after the ball is snapped. In order to do this, he must key the linemen in front of him and to either side. We use the term "get the big picture" when teaching the keys and reactions to blocking patterns.

(4) *Block Protection*—In order to protect himself from blockers, a lineman must develop the ability to use his hands, forearms, and shoulders. We want the linemen to use their shoulders if the blocker is coming off the line above the waist and use their hands if the blocker is low. We always want the defense to get up under the offensive blocker's pads if possible. If our linemen can accomplish this objective, we will win most of the battles.

(5) *Feet*—For a defensive lineman to play well, he must develop the ability to deliver a blow and at the same time move his feet as he sheds the blocker. Only when teaching isolated components of a technique should a drill be used that does not involve quick foot movement.

(6) *Pursuit*—This area of defense is often overlooked when drills are set up because a number of coaches do not believe pursuit can be taught. We want out linemen to understand the correct pursuit angles and to be able to take the quickest route to the ball.

(7) *Tackling*—The most important phase of defense is tackling. If a defensive lineman has the desire to get to the ball and tackle, he can overcome a weakness in another area of technique. Tackling drills should be incorporated into each practice session.

These seven checkpoints are taken into consideration when drills are set up for practice. Whenever we find that a defensive lineman is not playing his position effectively, we go over each one of these points in order to isolate the problem and then set up a drill in order to correct the fault.

6 POINT HIT DRILL

(A) Objective: To teach the correct use of the upper part of the body when delivering a blow with the shoulder and forearm.

(B) Equipment: A two- or seven-man sled.

(C) Explanation: The players assume a position on hands and knees, six to eight inches from each pad on the sled. The coach must designate which shoulder is to be used before the beginning of the drill. In command, the players must explode with the shoulder and forearm into the pad. The knees must never leave the turf. The back should be arched and the hips tucked as the shoulder and flipper reach the pad at the same time.

4 POINT HIT DRILL

(A) Objective: To develop the ability of a defensive lineman to deliver a blow with his legs and upper body.

(B) Equipment: A two- or seven-man sled.

(C) Explanation: Each player should align himself two to three feet from the pad. We want the lineman to explode with his legs, tuck the tail, and coordinate the shoulder and forearm as he delivers a blow. Some common faults are failure to keep the head up, hitting with a broken flipper (shoulder making contact before forearm can be brought up), and making contact with only the forearm.

HIT AND SLIDE DRILL (See Figure 10-1)

(A) Objective: To develop the ability of a lineman to deliver a blow and move his feet as he works across a blocker's face.

(B) Equipment: One seven-man sled.

(C) Explanation: All players begin on the left side of the sled facing the pads. The first lineman assumes a stance and on command hits with the right shoulder and flipper. As the blow is passed, the player must shuffle his feet and work across the pad. Once he comes across the pad, the player must work on all fours to the next pad, where the procedure is repeated. When the last pad has been passed, the lineman should roll out and break down into a hitting position. After all players have used the right shoulder, they should repeat the drill using the left shoulder. Points to emphasize are: deliver a blow, move the feet, stay on all fours, bounce across the pad, and quickness. We believe this drill helps our linemen to play the kick-out block because they develop the feel of delivering a blow and working to the inside.

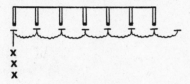

Figure 10-1

1 ON 1 DRILL (See Figure 10-2)

(A) Objective: To teach a defensive lineman how to read the offensive blocker and the proper reaction to each block that is shown.

(B) Equipment: None.

(C) Explanation: Players are paired off according to the position they play, and they face each other from a distance of two to three feet. One line is designated as the offensive blockers. The offense must show four types of blocks: the kick-out or drive block, the reach block, the down block, and the drop back pass block. The offensive blockers can move whenever they want since there is no snap count given by the coach. The defense should receive at least two repetitions of each block they must master. After eight repetitions, the players change positions and the drill is repeated.

This is an excellent drill for young players since they must be able to play these four basic blocks effectively in order to contribute to the defense. A safety factor to be considered is that each pair of players needs plenty of room in which to work. The coach should move from player to player, correcting faults and keeping the drill moving at a fast pace.

Figure 10-2

PASS RUSH DRILL

(A) Objective: To teach the basic drop back pass rush techniques to defensive linemen.

(B) Equipment: Two bell bottom dummies, a stopwatch, and a plastic cone.

(C) Explanation: An offensive and a defensive lineman align themselves between the bags. The player on defense will be given a technique to play; i.e., a 0, 2, 3, 5, or 9. The coach should check for the correct stance and alignment of this particular technique before the drill is commenced.

     The offensive lineman will move on his own count once the coach gives the command for the drill to start. The defensive lineman must beat the blocker in three seconds, as timed by the coach. In order to make this drill competitive, a point system can be established, and the winner is the player who accomplishes his objective in three out of five attempts.

     Coaching points for the defensive linemen are: get as close to the line of scrimmage as possible without being offside, move on movement, and put pressure on the blocker before he can get set up. One other very important point to stress to the defense is that after pressure has been applied you must grab and pull the blocker forward and roll the correct arm over the opponent's helmet.

WHIRL DRILL (See Figure 10-3)

(A) Objective: To improve the ability of defensive linemen to read movement and step with the correct foot while delivering a blow with the shoulder and forearm.

(B) Equipment: None.

(C) Explanation: A defensive lineman is in a three- or four-point stance between two offensive blockers and two feet away from each man. On the command "Ready," the blockers assume a stance. On his own, the blocker to the left side fires out on the defense. This player must react by stepping with his right foot, dropping his hips slightly, and hitting up under the blocker's pads with his right shoulder and forearm. As soon as the hit is made, the defensive player scrambles back to the starting position and the procedure is repeated to the left side. As soon as two rapid hits have been made, the group rotates clockwise. The group crabs quickly to the starting position with another lineman on defense. The drill continues until all linemen have progressed through the exercise.

Figure 10-3

STUNT DRILL

(A) Objective: To develop the correct relationships between defensive linemen when executing stunts from different alignments.

(B) Equipment: Six or seven pop-up dummies. (The number will depend upon the formation desired.) Stand-up dummies may also be used.

(C) Explanation: The offense must have a complete backfield in order to run the particular formations and plays the defense will see in the upcoming game. The offense should have diagrams, numbered from one to fifteen, of the plays to be run. The quarterback will show these plays to the backs in the huddle and give the snap count. Meanwhile, the defensive coach who has a list of game-plan stunts should give the defensive call in the huddle. The play is run with quick movement but no contact as the coach checks the assignments of all linemen on defense.

7 ON 5 DRILL

(A) Objective: To teach the defensive line how to read and react to the different blocks that they will face against the upcoming opponent.

(B) Equipment: One football.

(C) Explanation: The offense has seven players lined up in a two tight end formation. The defense has a nose guard, two tackles, and two ends. The coach stands behind the defense and through the use of hand signals points out the different blocks for each offensive player. On the coach's command, the offensive linemen execute their assignments. This drill should be done at half speed until all blocking combinations have been shown to the defense. It should then be run at full speed in order to perfect game-type reactions. A quarterback should be used to take the snap and give the defensive ends flow.

9 ON 7 DRILL (Front Drill)

(A) Objective: To coordinate the play of the linebackers and defensive linemen against the ground game of the upcoming opponents.

(B) Equipment: None.

(C) Explanation: The offense must consist of everyone but the wide receivers. This team will use the ten favorite running plays of the opposition in no certain order. The defense will be given the down, distance, and position of the ball on the field. The Sam linebacker will make the defensive call and break the huddle. Both linebackers must check the formation as the offense breaks the huddle and make any adjustments or calls that are deemed necessary. This drill should be done at full speed in the spring and early fall, but as the season gets under way it should be full speed only five out of fifteen plays.

LINEBACKER DRILLS

A linebacker is exactly what the term implies: he backs the defensive line. The linebacker is neither a lineman nor a defensive back; he must play the run as tough as a nose guard or tackle and cover on passes as well as the strong safety.

Linebackers must master the basic fundamentals of one defense before moving to stunts of multiple defenses. These fundamentals are the ability to deliver a blow, shed the blocker, pursue, and tackle. The drills that we use to accomplish these objectives are discussed in this section.

2 POINT HIT DRILL

(A) Objective: To develop the ability of a linebacker to deliver a blow and move his feet.

(B) Equipment: A two-man sled.

(C) Explanation: Two linebackers assume a two-point stance in a "hitting" position, one foot from the pads. On the coach's command "Hit," the linebackers deliver a blow to the pads with their shoulders and forearms. The coach should stress exploding out of the hips and legs, with the shoulder and forearm making contact at the same instant. After delivering three blows to the sled, the players shuffle quickly to the outside, remaining in a good hitting position. The players alternate lines after they have completed the drill.

SHED DRILL (See Figure 10-4)

(A) Objective: To develop the ability of a linebacker to shed blockers and make the tackle.

(B) Equipment: One football and two bags.

(C) Explanation: A linebacker is facing a line of two blockers and a ball carrier, who are lined up in a single file three yards apart between the bags. The distance from the first blocker to the defensive player should be no more than four yards. On command, the first blocker should drive for the linebacker's right shoulder, make contact, and move to the outside. The second blocker should drive for the left shoulder, make contact, and move to the outside. The ball carrier should move straight ahead and break to one side or the other. The backer must hit and shuck both blockers, first with the right shoulder and then with the left, and tackle the ball carrier.

Figure 10-4

FAKE AND BREAK DRILL

(A) Objective: To develop the ability of a linebacker to tackle in the open field.

(B) Equipment: One football.

(C) Explanation: A linebacker is facing a runner at a distance of seven yards in a good hitting position. The runner moves forward at full speed until he is within three yards of the backer and then is allowed to make one fake and break in the opposite direction. The linebacker must keep his eyes open, get the helmet on the ball, and explode with his legs as he hits up and through the runner's legs. After each tackle, the players rotate lines until each linebacker has tackled four times.

READ DRILL (See Figure 10-5)

(A) Objective: To teach linebackers to key properly, to work behind the line of scrimmage to the point of attack, and to fill or scrape according to the defensive call.

(B) Equipment: Seven bell-bottom dummies.

(C) Explanation: The offense consists of the dummies, which represent the offensive line, a quarterback, and a set of running backs. If the linebackers are reading the guards as the primary key, two players must be used to show the different blocks. The dummies are set up to show the different holes along the line of scrimmage. The coach should prepare diagrams of the plays to be run by the offense so as to get as many repetitions as possible in a short time. The coach should know which play is coming up next in order to check the techniques of the backers against that particular play. For example, if a 50 Strong Slant is called in the huddle and run flow

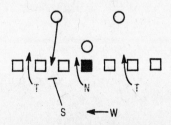

Figure 10-5

shows in the off-tackle area to the strong side, Sam must step up and fill between the tackle and nose guard. All calls that are included in the game plan will be used in this drill against the opponent's plays. Each linebacker must be exposed to these plays and the different calls at least three times during the week preceding a game.

DROP DRILL (See Figure 10-6)

(A) Objective: To teach the linebackers to read pass or run and to develop correct techniques of underneath pass coverage.

(B) Equipment: Three cones, two bags, and two footballs.

(C) Explanation: The offensive set-up will consist of a coach, who acts as the quarterback; two bags, which simulate the guards; two running backs; a tight end; and two wide receivers. The bags are placed three to three and a half yards apart, with the quarterback inside the bags. The cones are placed fourteen to seventeen yards from the ball in the middle and curl areas.

The coach calls the formation and play in the huddle and the routes to be run. The backers must recognize the formation, read the play, and react. Coaching points to emphasize are: read through the guard to the near back to determine pass or run

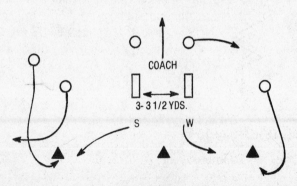

Figure 10-6

flow, the backers should pick up the routes of the receivers as they move to their responsibilities, and break on the ball.

SECONDARY DRILLS

ON 1 WEAVE DRILL (See Figure 10-7)

A) Objective: To develop the ability of a defensive back to change directions with a receiver, improve body control, and run with a receiver once the final move has been made.

B) Equipment: None.

C) Explanation: A defensive back lines up eight to twelve yards from a receiver. The receiver comes off the line of scrimmage and breaks to the outside at an angle, runs five to seven yards, and then reverses the procedure. The receiver makes four breaks and runs a streak pattern. The defensive man must maintain a cushion and the correct position as he changes direction with the receiver and runs with him on the streak pattern. The coach throws the ball after the fourth cut, and both players must go for the ball.

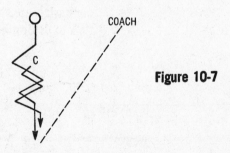

COACH

Figure 10-7

STRETCH DRILL (See Figure 10-8)

(A) Objective: To improve and develop the ability of a defensive back to get a jump on the ball and cover a large area of the field.

(B) Equipment: None.

(C) Explanation: Three backs are lined up twenty yards from the coach, with one on each hash mark and one in the middle of the field.

Start the drill by slapping the ball, taking one step back, and throwing to one of the backs on a hash mark. The man in the middle must break as the coach starts the throwing motion.

The receiver should tip the ball toward the sideline in order to give the man breaking a chance for an interception. The distance the three backs are lined up from the coach will vary depending on the speed of your players and how hard the coach throws to the man on the hash marks.

This drill should be used early in fall workouts and in spring practice in order to place emphasis on the amount of ground that can be covered if a back breaks on the ball correctly. This drill is especially good for young secondary players. This drill should also be used by the linebackers.

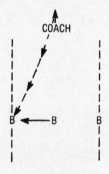

Figure 10-8

ROTATION DRILL (See Figure 10-9)

(A) Objective: To teach the techniques of proper rotation and the elimination of false steps on all coverages.

(B) Equipment: None.

(C) Explanation: A full secondary is set up facing three receivers and the coach, who acts as the quarterback. The coach can huddle with the receivers and give instructions on whether to block or run a pass pattern. The coach should take four to five steps down the line to stimulate a run play. If a pass play has been called, the coach must come straight back or toward one of the cornerbacks at an angle to stimulate a sprint out pass.

Each coverage that is included in the game plan for the upcoming opponent must be included in this drill. This rotation drill should be done at least three times in the week of practice preceding the game. This drill is also excellent for teaching the basic principles of rotation to young players when the coach uses only one or two basic calls.

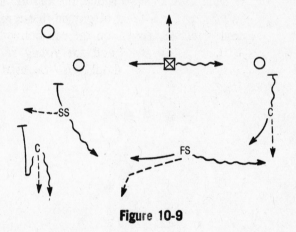

Figure 10-9

SKELETON PASS DRILL (See Figure 10-10)

(A) Objective: To develop the ability of the defensive secondary to react as a coordinated unit against the threat of run or pass.

(B) Equipment: Five cones.

(C) Explanation: The cones are set up to simulate the five offensive linemen. The remainder of the offense will consist of the quarterback, two running backs, and three receivers. The defense can also add linebackers and/or ends to this drill in order to give underneath coverage.

The plays should be run under close scrutiny of at least one offensive and one defensive coach. Both units should strive hard to perfect techniques involved in the passing game.

In order to make this drill more competitive and remove the drudgery of practice, a point system can be devised in order to determine a winner for the day. A specific number of points should be awarded to the offense for short and long completions. The defense should be rewarded for interceptions and incompletions. A stopwatch should be used to determine the amount of time the quarterback has to throw. Points should also be awarded to the defense if they cover the receivers past this alloted time.

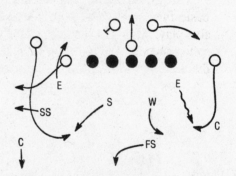

Figure 10-10

TEAM DRILLS

FALCON DRILL (See Figure 10-11)

(A) Objective: To teach the basic fundamentals of blocking, defensive line play, ball carrying techniques, pursuit, and open field tackling.

(B) Equipment: Two bell bottom dummies; one football.

(C) Explanation: The offense will consist of one blocker, a ball carrier, a quarterback, and a center, although the quarterback and center will not be directly involved in the action. The defense should have a lineman on the line of scrimmage and either a linebacker or a defensive back ten to twelve yards from the ball. There will be two dummies placed on the twenty yard line two yards apart. The linemen will line up on the ball with the running back directly behind the offensive blocker and four yards deep. On the snap, the back receives the ball from the quarterback as the blocker attempts to carry the defense in any direction. If the ball carrier breaks through the bags, the defensive player on the ten yard line can attempt to tackle him. The defensive lineman must pursue and try to help on the tackle. The running back should strive to cross the goal line anyway possible.

In my opinion, the falcon drill teaches the basic fundamentals of both offensive and defensive play. This drill should be used extensively in spring practice and early fall. During the season, the use of this drill should be limited.

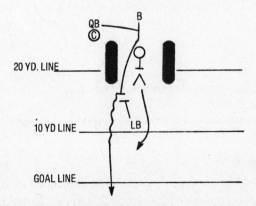

Figure 10-11

BUTT AND STRING UP

(A) Objective: To develop coordination between all positions on defense and to practice the defensive checks and calls against the opponent's formations and plays.

(B) Equipment: None.

(C) Explanation: This drill is nothing more than a controlled scrimmage. The defense must play the blocks full speed and react to the ball at full speed, with the first man butting the ball carrier and the remainder of the defense closing in to touch the runner.

The defensive coaches should organize this drill carefully. Diagrams of all formations, plays, pass routes, and blocking assignments should be drawn up for the offense and numbered consecutively. The defensive coaches should meet and plan what defense is to be checked out against each play. A script should be made out and be in the possession of each coach so coaches can check the players at the point of attack and know what defense is called against each offensive play. The script will have the formation, plays, and defensive calls written on it.

During this drill, the coach who calls the defensive signals should be on the sideline and communicate with the Sam linebacker through hand signals after referring to the script. The remainder of the staff should not be close to the defensive huddle. This drill, except for correction of mistakes by the coaches, should put the players on their own in a situation that most closely resembles a game-type situation.

INDEX